YOUNG

PALESTINIANS

SPEAK

Israel, Occupied West Bank and neighboring countries

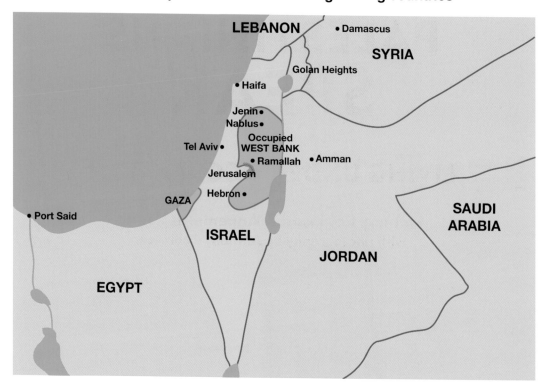

YOUNG
PALESTINIANS
SPEAK

LIVING UNDER OCCUPATION

Anthony Robinson & Annemarie Young
with photography by Anthony Robinson

Interlink Books

An imprint of Interlink Publishing Group, Inc.
Northampton, Massachusetts

Dedication

This book is dedicated to all young Palestinians, particularly those whose stories and words appear in the book, and to all young people living under difficult, life-threatening or constraining circumstances.

First published in 2017 by
INTERLINK BOOKS
An imprint of Interlink Publishing Group, Inc.
46 Crosby Street, Northampton, Massachusetts 01060
www.interlinkbooks.com

Text and maps copyright © Anthony Robinson and
        Annemarie Young, 2017
Photographs © Anthony Robinson, 2017

Library of Congress Cataloging-in-Publication Data
Names: Robinson, Anthony, 1949 September 8– author. |
        Young, Annemarie, author.
Title: Young Palestinians speak : living under occupation /
        by Anthony Robinson and Annemarie Young.
Description: Northampton, MA : Interlink Books, an
        imprint of Interlink Publishing Group, Inc., 2017. |
        Includes bibliographical references.
Identifiers: LCCN 2016042874 | ISBN 9781566560153
Subjects: LCSH: Arab-Israeli conflict—Juvenile literature. |
        Palestinian Arabs—Juvenile literature. | Children,
        Palestinian Arab—Interviews—Juvenile literature. |
        West Bank—History—Juvenile literature. | Gaza
        Strip—History—Juvenile literature.
Classification: LCC DS119.7 .R576 2017 | DDC
        956.95/3045—dc23
LC record available at https://lccn.loc.gov/2016042874

Printed and bound in Korea

Thanks

Our gratitude goes first to the children and young people who talked to us about their lives, and shared their thoughts and feelings with us.

We would also like to thank all those who offered us help along the way. It has been a long, and at times, twisty road. These people are too numerous to mention individually, but we hope they understand the importance of the part they have played and how grateful we are.

Our particular thanks go to:
Those at the Tamer Institute for Community Education, without whose logistical and practical support our journey would not have been possible, particularly Juwana and Ruba. And to Jehan Helou and Mary Fasheh, for doing their best to facilitate one of our more awkward encounters!

Our special thanks to Samar Qutob, for her tireless and selfless support as well as her constant encouragement.

Raja Shehadeh for his initial encouragement, for his incisive comments on an early draft of the introduction, and for his support throughout the project.

Beverley Naidoo for her perceptive comments on the text.

Our publisher, Michel Moushabeck, for having the courage to take on the project.

Ann Childs, our editor, for her insightful and helpful comments and her meticulous editing.

Pam Fontes-May, the designer, for her stylish and imaginative designs and solutions, and for listening!

Giles Aston, for his skill, professional expertise and generosity in compiling the maps.

Finally, we would like to thank the Society of Authors for their generous support of this project with a grant from the Authors' Foundation.

CONTENTS

WHAT IS THIS BOOK ABOUT? 7
WHAT IS OCCUPATION? 10
What does occupation mean?
What does occupation look like?

LIFE UNDER OCCUPATION 13
Israeli settlements within the Occupied
    Territories
How does occupation affect human rights?
What citizenship do the Palestinians have?
Poverty in Gaza and the Occupied
    Territories
Education
Housing and land ownership
Justice and the law
Land
Water
The Separation Wall and its effects
Checkpoints and other obstacles to
    movement
What does "security" mean?

HOW THIS AFFECTS
PALESTINIANS TODAY 24
RAMALLAH 26
Ramallah City and the Qalandia
    Checkpoint
Howari Bo Medyan School, Ramallah
The Tamer Institute, Ramallah

JENIN 40
Animation Workshop in the Old Jenin
    Library

NABLUS 46
A walk in the Old City
An apartment in Nablus

QATTANA 50
The House behind the Wall: A Special Case
Back in the village of Qattana

SEBASTIYA 56
Children from the village
Ahmed, local farmer and volunteer

GAZA 62
Talking to children in Gaza—before the
    July 2014 bombardments
The Tamer coordinators
Interviews in 2015

BEIT UR 76
Beit Ur School
The children's stories

HEBRON 84
The Cordoba School: a school under siege
The Hebron Youth Development Resource
    Center

BURJ AL LUQ LUQ—
EAST JERUSALEM   98

TO OUR READERS:
THE YOUNG MATTER   106

TIMELINE OF THE PALESTINIAN–
ISRAELI CONFLICT   108

REFERENCES   113

WHAT IS THIS BOOK ABOUT?

Young Palestinians want to be heard.

We have, for many years, been concerned with giving children who are denied a voice a chance to be heard. This is the reason we have published books on refugee children, street children, and now this book about and by young Palestinians.

Why do we feel this way? We believe that everybody should be allowed a voice. Being heard means you matter, and we all want to matter. Palestinian children and young people live in an occupied country. Can you imagine what it is like living in a country where soldiers are ever-present, where you cannot move about freely, where you are not wanted?

This book is our attempt to give these young people an opportunity to speak.

Much of what you will read are the stories of young Palestinians, told in their own voices. As you read their words, you will see that what they want is a stable family life, security where they live, the freedom to move around their country, safety, and space in which to grow up and dream of a future. They are just like young people everywhere. It is only the circumstances of their lives that are so different. We hope that these stories, and the occupation's background, will give you an idea of what it is like for them to live in their present circumstances.

SAMIA an 11-year-old girl from Gaza told us: "...We are suffering here in Gaza because of the occupation. We have dreams like other children ... children's dreams. I would tell about what it's like living in an occupied country and how kids suffer and dream of living in safety."

But we do not want you to think of the Palestinians as victims; our aim is to help you understand the situation. As Raja Shehadeh has said: "No one is helped by being reduced to the status of victim. Palestinians don't need to be pitied or viewed as unfortunates who deserve assistance and relief. They need people to understand their cause and work with them to bring justice and peace to their war-battered land."

With the help of the Tamer Institute for Community Education, we visited and talked to children and young people, and some older ones, in towns and villages all around the Occupied Territories: Ramallah, Jenin, Nablus, Sebastiya, Qattana, Beit Ur, Hebron, and East Jerusalem, and we held video conferences with children and young people in Gaza. We asked them to tell us what life is like, and to tell us about their hopes and dreams. We learned a great deal and are grateful to them all.

Because context is crucial to understanding any situation, the book begins with a short introduction, which explains what occupation is and how it affects the Palestinians living in the Occupied Territories. This is followed by nine sections, each one focusing on one of the places we visited. It is a map of stories: each section begins with a brief introduction followed by the young people's stories. They tell their stories in their own words because we believe that the children's true thoughts and feelings matter, and are best represented as they are expressed. At the end of the book there is a timeline showing the main events that led up to the occupation, and a list of references and other information.

For us, this project was both a physical journey to places and a journey towards understanding. It was about crossing borders, being there, and reporting back.

WHAT IS THIS BOOK ABOUT?

We hope that what you read here will help to give you an understanding of these children's lives and of their hopes for a future lived in freedom and safety.

Anthony Robinson
and Annemarie Young
Cambridge, England

WHAT IS OCCUPATION?

WHAT DOES OCCUPATION MEAN?

Occupation is the settlement or taking and controlling of an area by military force. It is an act of possession against the wishes of the people who live there.

The area of Palestinian territory known as the West Bank has been occupied by Israel since the end of the Six-Day War in June, 1967. This area is also referred to as the Occupied Territories. (The Gaza Strip was also occupied until 2005.)

WHAT DOES OCCUPATION LOOK LIKE?

These four maps show the changes—the loss of Palestinian land—between 1946 and 2014. Palestinian land has continued to shrink, with the creation and expansion of illegal settlements within the Occupied Territories, and the loss of land associated with the building and maintenance of the Separation Wall.

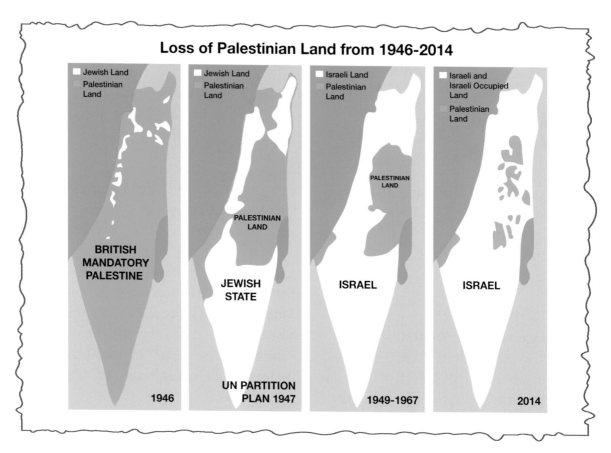

Loss of Palestinian Land from 1946-2014

Jewish Land
Palestinian Land

BRITISH MANDATORY PALESTINE

1946

Jewish Land
Palestinian Land

PALESTINIAN LAND

JEWISH STATE

UN PARTITION PLAN 1947

Israeli Land
Palestinian Land

PALESTINIAN LAND

ISRAEL

1949-1967

Israeli and Israeli Occupied Land

Palestinian Land

ISRAEL

2014

WHAT IS OCCUPATION?

THE OSLO PEACE ACCORDS OF 1993 AND THE CREATION OF AREAS A, B, & C

After the 1993 Oslo Accords, the final status of the West Bank was put on hold, to be decided some time in the future. This still has not happened. In the meantime, the control of the West Bank was divided between Israel and Palestine, through the creation of three different types of "areas": A, B, and C.

Area A, which makes up 18% of the land in the West Bank and is home to 55% of West Bank Palestinians, was put under the control of the Palestinian Authority (PA). Although Area A is officially under the control of the PA, the Israeli military can enter this area "for security reasons" at any time.

Area B, 22% of the land and 41% of the Palestinians, was put under joint Israeli-Palestinian control—the PA has the civil authority and the Israelis have control of security.

Area C is the area which causes the Palestinians most difficulty. It makes up 60% of the land and 4% of the Palestinians, and is under full Israeli control. There are 150,000 Palestinians

Map of areas A, B and C for the Occupied Territories

living in Area C, compared to 400,000 Jewish settlers living in 124 "official" settlements and 100 illegal "outposts."

Area C contains all of the Israeli settlements, settler roads, security buffer zones, strategic areas, and Israeli military bases and zones. The places in the West Bank that make up most of Area C are the Jordan Valley, East Jerusalem, and the Judean desert.

While the majority of the Palestinian population lives in Areas A and B, much of the land around these Palestinian built-up areas, villages, and cities is defined as Area C. Therefore, many Palestinian communities have lost farmland—vital to the economy of many villages—as well as the land that their communities would naturally expand into as the population increases. The Israeli military retains full control of the land, roads, water, airspace, security and borders for the land in Area C.

Life is made almost impossible for any Palestinians living in or near Area C because of the complex bureaucratic systems that exist. Palestinians in Area C need a permit from the Israelis in order to repair their own homes and to build new homes on their own land, to access water, and to access their own farmland. These permits are often refused.

Sometimes you will see corrugated tin roofs camouflaged with plastic covering; this is because building a roof out of metal counts as "building a second story" in the Israeli system. And of course, they would need a nearly impossible-to-get permit for that.

"Breathing is the only thing we don't need a permit for—yet!" Ahmed, local farmer and activist from Sebastiya, told us.

WHAT ARE THE SETTLEMENTS AND "OUTPOSTS"?

Settlements are Jewish-only communities built by Israel within the Occupied Territories. These "official" settlements are illegal under international humanitarian law – they violate Article 49 of the Fourth Geneva Convention, 1949, which explicitly prohibits an occupying power from transferring any part of its civilian population into territory it occupies. But they are authorized by the Israeli government, and receive the same benefits and services as towns within Israel's pre-1967 borders.

In addition to the settlements officially sanctioned by the Israeli government, there are also approximately 100 "outpost" settlements in the West Bank. Although built without official approval—and considered illegal even by the Israeli government—they receive financial support from government ministries and agencies, and most have state funded protection and access to water, electricity, and other services.

12

Muath, a 20-year-old man we met at the Tamer Institute for Community Education in Ramallah, told us:

"Yeah, the world thinks of Palestinians as terrorists. But we are just people trying to live here. Living in a prison, with no freedom of movement. We have to ask permission, we need ID in our own country."

The impact of occupation on political, social, and economic life is felt daily. The occupation has an effect on education, housing, access to water and roads, justice, land ownership, and, as Muath points out above, on freedom of movement.

Samia, a 12-year-old girl in Gaza, said: *"The occupation. It fills our lives. We cannot escape it."*

Israel controls all Palestinian borders, air space, water, tax revenues, all imports and exports, and all movement between towns and cities. And Israel alone issues the identity cards that determine where Palestinians can live, work, and visit.

Overall, living standards and conditions, especially in Gaza, are far below those enjoyed by Israelis who live in Israel or in the illegal settlements of the Occupied Territories.

ISRAELI SETTLEMENTS WITHIN THE OCCUPIED TERRITORIES

Israel has been building settlements for Israelis in the Occupied Territories since the 1967 Six-Day War. The international community, both through the United Nations and individual countries, considers the establishment of Israeli settlements in the Israeli-occupied territories illegal under international law.

The settlements are effectively towns, containing everything you would expect in a town. They are usually built on hilltops, and surrounded by walls and fences which encroach on Palestinian farmland. They are also invariably protected by Israeli security forces and do not come under Palestinian law. They are connected to Israel through a system of roads which are out of bounds to Palestinians.

HOW DOES OCCUPATION AFFECT HUMAN RIGHTS?

There is no freedom of movement.

The right to free speech and free assembly are seriously restricted.

There is arrest and imprisonment without charge or trial. This includes children.

Houses can be searched without a warrant.

Palestinians in the West Bank cannot vote for the Israeli government, even though it controls their lives.

Yara, a 10-year-old girl from the Howari Medyan School, Ramallah, said: *"We should be able to live and be happy with our lives. I am from Gaza, but our family is not allowed to return. The Israelis won't give us permits. My father lived in Ramallah before, so the family came here, but now we are not allowed to go back."*

WHAT CITIZENSHIP DO THE PALESTINIANS HAVE?

Because the Palestinians do not have a state of their own, they cannot have Palestinian citizenship in the same way that you can have American, British, Spanish, or Argentinian citizenship. The Palestinian Authority has been allowed to give Palestinians who live in the areas under their authority a Palestinian Authority Passport/Travel Document. But the Israeli government imposes restrictions by requiring Palestinians to get a permit from the Israeli authorities if they want to move around different areas or enter Israel. Many people are not granted the permits.

The situation for the descendants of Palestinians who were refugees after 1947/1948 and 1967 is even more difficult. Millions of Palestinians remain stateless refugees in Jordan, Lebanon, Syria, and elsewhere, having escaped the violence of 1947/48 and 1967. They are unable to return to their homes and were forced into over-crowded camps in Palestine or abroad. Many are still there. The United Nations have said they should be allowed to return. Israel says no. They are stateless. Citizens of nowhere.

Abdul Aziz, a 16-year-old boy from Jenin told us: *"My father came from Nouris, a '1948' village, one that was taken over by the Israelis. They demolished it and everybody was forced into the Jenin Camp. My mom was also from a village near Jenin, but she escaped to Jordan. They were more welcome there than in their own country. They lost their homeland."*

POVERTY IN GAZA AND THE OCCUPIED TERRITORIES

The Gaza Strip, although no longer occupied (since 2005), is still surrounded and sealed off from the rest of the world—by land, air, and sea. It is, in effect, the world's largest open-air prison. Its borders are controlled by Israel. Its people have no right of access to the West Bank, to employment, families, better medical facilities, and higher education. In short, to their own country. The attacks by Israel have left much of Gaza without housing, and have increased poverty. Health issues have worsened because of water contamination and unfixable public utilities, including electricity and water treatment plants. The July/August 2014 attacks on Gaza have made a very bad situation significantly worse for the civilian population.

Nour, a 14-year-old boy from Gaza, told us: *"It's not living. We survive. Some families are separated and might never see each other again. It's too crowded here. There is no space and not enough housing for families. Everybody gets tense, fights start. We are prisoners and have no control over our lives."*

In the Occupied Territories many people are dependent on international food aid. Unemployment rates in the West Bank are high, around 20%, and in Gaza about 40%. As discussed above, living conditions in Gaza are also very poor due to over-crowding, war damage, and difficulties bringing in building material and medicines.

EDUCATION

Within the Occupied Territories, Palestinian schools suffer from under-funding compared to the schools of the illegal Jewish settlements. Education in Palestine is controlled by the Palestinian Ministry of Education and Higher Education. However, they do not have the funds that the State of Israel has. The situation is even worse in Gaza, where funds are largely taken up with rebuilding schools after Israeli bombing raids. In addition, Israel makes sure its illegal settlements are well-funded as a way of

Beit Ur school is surrounded on three sides by a wall, and an Israeli highway on the fourth.

making them attractive to settlers and their families. The Israeli military can and do harass and close Palestinian schools. Israeli settlers often abuse, threaten, and attack Palestinian schoolchildren. Many Palestinian students must pass through military checkpoints to get to school. There is no guarantee they will be allowed to pass, so they often miss school.

Haneen, a 14-year-old girl from Biet Ur School: *"We get afraid. The occupation is everywhere. The settlers make us afraid. They come to our school with their weapons. It's scary … They make so much noise whenever they like … we can't study."*

Palestinian schools have also been attacked by the Israeli military. The United Nations Educational, Scientific and Cultural Organization (UNESCO) has documented that in just one period, 2003-2005, the Israeli military caused $5 million dollars in damage to Palestinian schools. The damage to Palestinian schools in the most recent Gaza conflict has yet to be determined, but the damage to schools, housing, hospitals, and other major infrastructure was considerable.

HOUSING AND LAND OWNERSHIP AND DEMOLITIONS

Shahed is a 10-year-old-girl, and Mira is an 11-year-old girl; both are from Silwan, Jerusalem. They told us: *"Our parents get really upset when homes are built or changed about in our area without permission, by Israeli settlers. When soldiers enter Al-Aqsa Mosque and arrest people … when other 'accidents' happen there. We have to get permission for any changes to our homes, but settlers can do what they like."*

Mira said: *"It was the same near Ramallah too, my parents said."*

Taseem, a young woman who is a volunteer worker at the Burj Luq Luq Social Center, East Jerusalem, told us: *"It is one rule for them, another for us…For example, in 2011, the Israelis wanted to take over parts of Silwan. They got a court order saying it was okay, but there was a huge protest, by many Israelis too, and it was stopped. But for how long?"*

Israel makes it impossible for Palestinian families to build or improve property. The policy of the Israeli authorities is to encourage settlers, tacitly or otherwise, to build and expand, while Palestinians are prevented from building new houses or even from repairing their current homes.

All building work requires expensive permits, which the Israeli authorities rarely grant to Palestinians. Many are forced to build without permits because of cramped living conditions or deterioration and structural issues. This means that the authorities can and do demolish these structures as they do not comply with the regulations.

Very recently, in September 2016, Israeli authorities carried out a large number of demolitions in occupied East Jerusalem and the West Bank. These included the destruction of two family apartment buildings, a classroom, a restaurant, four water cisterns, and parts of a home. In one of the demolitions, sixteen Palestinians, including a number of children, were left homeless after bulldozers demolished two houses in East Jerusalem in the middle of the night. The Israeli forces arrived at 3 a.m. and forcibly evacuated the families from their apartments without letting them retrieve their belongings. The owners had tried and failed to obtain construction permits since 2010, forcing them to build the two residences without licenses.

Shamad, a 13-year-old-boy from Gaza: "Israeli forces stole lots of land from Beit Hannoun here in Gaza. Our family land was stolen..."

In contrast, illegal settlements continue to grow, all over the Occupied Territories. Israel also refuses to recognize the Palestinian rights to many homes, towns, and villages taken just before the State of Israel was declared in 1948.

Mohammad, a Nablus shopkeeper, said: "They want all the land. They want us to leave. But where would we go? To Jordan, Syria? No, this is our home...my home. What can we do? They control us."

JUSTICE AND THE LAW

During much of the occupation, Palestinians have had no right to civil law. If accused by the Israelis, they face military courts. By contrast, Israeli settlers in the Occupied Territories are considered to be Israeli citizens and have rights under Israeli law, but are not subject to Palestinian law.

Qais, a 10-year-old boy from Balata* refugee camp said: "I get frightened sometimes. It's when the Israelis come once a week to pray at the Tomb of Jusef (Joseph). They are from the settlements. The soldiers come with them, for security they say, and they shoot in the air. They are frightening. Also, they can just arrest you..."

*Balata, next to Nablus, is where 30,000 people live in less than 10 square miles, or 0.25 square kilometers.

My father was arrested ten years ago. He had no trial. He was in prison for 4–5 years, for political reasons—during the first Intifada, in 1987."

Hamad, a 12-year-old boy from the Balata camp told us: "... We all live in one room—nine people. I would get rid of Israeli guns in our lives. They come into Balata every day and make a lot of noise and trouble. They come in cars and sometimes in tanks and they often arrest people. There is no trial. No law for us. We all stay inside when this happens. We are terrified."

Palestinian children can be prosecuted and jailed from the age of 12 under military law.

Lina, a 10-year-old girl from Sebastiya: "... they took my 14-year old cousin away once, for two days ... the soldiers didn't tell him why. They brought him back in the middle of the night ... at 2 AM. He won't talk about it. They like to disturb us. All the families were angry and upset."

Since 1967, more than 650,000 Palestinians have served time in prison—this represents about 40% of today's male population.

LAND
Ahmed, a village elder from Sebastiya, told us: "... The settlers are always uprooting our olive trees, and in 2012 they began pumping raw sewage onto our fields. Those fields down there, right in front of us. It started to affect our olive and apricot trees."

According to Human Rights Watch, Israel now controls over 70% of the occupied West Bank (despite the official Areas). This includes land taken over for settlements, special military zones and parkland, and more land swallowed up by the construction of the Wall.

Tala, an 11-year-old boy from Sebastiya: "My parents worry about our land. We all do. In 2006, the settlement closest to us, Shave Shomron, put up a fence, which cut off some of our land. We couldn't farm..."

The Israeli state has built about 350 towns or villages on land that was lost to the Palestinians in the mass clearings that the Israelis carried out in 1947/48,

Israeli settlement seen from town of Sebastiya

before and after the setting up of the State of Israel in 1948. The Israelis say the land was deserted, the owners absent. They were absent because the Israelis refused to let them return. This policy has continued ever since. The number of settlements increased significantly after the occupation.

WATER

Access to water is another complex issue and, in a desert climate, a crucial one. Israel has effectively controlled water in the Occupied Territories and Gaza since 1967. Palestinian water has been diverted to the illegal Jewish settlements, and many Palestinians lack running water and must pay heavily for it to be delivered. This is not true in the settlements.

According to the World Bank, Palestinians have access to one-fifth of the resources of the shared Israeli-Palestinian groundwater resource. This is the only remaining water resource for the Palestinians, as well as one of the most important for Israel. This resource is replenished naturally mostly in the West Bank. Palestinians take about 20% of the "estimated potential" of the water resources that lie under both the West Bank and Israel. Israel takes out the remaining 80%.

The result is that Israeli settlements have swimming pools and green grass in every yard, while in Palestinian cities and villages, people can go for weeks without water in their homes and for their farms, especially during the summer.

In Gaza much of the water is polluted. This is the result of extensive war damage that cannot be repaired because of Israel's blockade on building materials coming into Gaza.

THE SEPARATION WALL AND ITS EFFECTS

The Separation Wall makes an already difficult life even harder for the Palestinians in the Occupied Territories.

Walls are not new in the West Bank. They surround all the illegal settlements, separating the occupiers from the

occupied. But Israel started building the Separation Wall, or Apartheid Wall as some call it, in 2002, saying it needed a wall to protect itself from Palestinian terrorism. Two-thirds of this huge concrete barrier runs through the West Bank, in places cutting through villages, towns, and cities.

Human Rights Watch estimates that on completion of the Wall, Palestinians will have lost another 9% of their land. In many places the Wall cuts into Palestinian land, obstructing access to their land and their work. This is just another way it is becoming extremely difficult for Palestinians to have a joined-up area in which to live and work, as the West Bank is pock-marked by obstacles, which make normal life and commerce impossible.

Muath: *"It's not normal to be a prisoner in your own country, to not be able to move around freely and not to have the opportunity to leave controlled areas ..."*

Biet Ur and Al Tireh are two villages about 8 miles, or 13 kilometers, from Ramallah. They are feeling the effects of the Wall on their education, freedom of movement, and safety. Hamaam Ismael, a 12-year-old boy from Biet Ur, told us: *"Our daily suffering is great, but it becomes worse every winter. We are forced to walk on foot for half an hour to reach school."*

Issa Ali Issa, the administrative manager of the Beit Ur School said: *"First, the Wall was built around our school, then the Occupation Forces imposed strong rules upon the students.*

Every now and then, additional 'actions' are taken against the school. Sometimes the Occupation Forces cut the water supply to the school. Recently, they narrowed the sand road that buses use to bring children to school. Now no bus can reach the school. They don't want us here."

The Wall makes economic development more difficult all over the West Bank. Crossing through the Wall requires a permit.

The Wall also goes through towns and cities, like Bethlehem, again separating Palestinians from each other. Going to work, to school, or to the hospital can often mean going through military checkpoints. A simple journey can then take all day or be stopped completely if access is denied at the checkpoint.

This severe restriction on freedom of movement has had serious effects on the Palestinian economy.

According to the United Nations, approximately 15,000 Palestinians have been forced to move because they could no longer live or work as a result of the construction of the Wall.

CHECKPOINTS AND OTHER OBSTACLES TO MOVEMENT

In the Occupied Territories, according to B'Tselem, an Israeli Human Rights Organization, many Israeli-built roads are only for Israelis and settlers. Some of the other roads require a Palestinian to have a permit. The Israeli road system crisscrosses the Occupied Territories in such a way that travel and connections in their own land is very difficult for Palestinians. To add to this, the separate Palestinian road system is mostly poor.

Bahan, a 14-year-old boy, a student of Biet Ur School, said: "*I get up early because I come to school on foot. I walk for 2 kilometers. I'm tired when I arrive. I come from the village over there, Tireh ... I have to come through a pipe, which was designed to carry water ...*"

Amhed, from Sebastiya: "*Slowly, slowly, the increase in Israeli checkpoints, barriers and restricted roads have made it too difficult to get here. The village is getting poorer because of this. Tourists used to come to look at our ancient sites.* *"

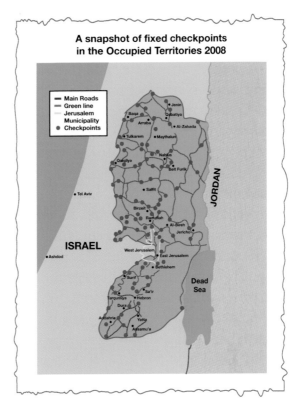

A snapshot of fixed checkpoints in the Occupied Territories 2008

It's too difficult now. They have stopped coming."

Checkpoints are just one of the many hurdles put in the way of Palestinians. Others include trenches, earth walls, partial checkpoints, road barriers, road gates, earth mounds, and "flying checkpoints" (these are put up suddenly, without warning).

The ancient site of Samaria-Sebaste is located here. These ruins dominate the hillside and are the remains from six successive cultures dating back 10,000 years.

Even without the Wall, Palestinians must pass through these mazes ... some have to go through them daily. The most infamous of these is the checkpoint at Qalandia. This separates Ramallah from southern Palestine, and northern Palestine from Jerusalem. Here, Palestinians can wait all day to cross, with no guarantees they will be allowed through.

While waiting to go through the Qalandia checkpoint in May, 2009, Brigid Keenan, attending a literary festival in Palestine, saw a family being turned back: "The husband was young but clearly very ill—there was a tube with blood in it coming out from his clothes, and his wife was practically carrying him. Her face was shiny with tears and their toddler was clinging to her legs as she walked."

Gaza is also enclosed by fences on the Israeli and Egyptian sides, from the air by the Israeli Air Force, and by Israeli gunboats at sea, making Israeli border control complete. Palestinians cannot travel outside Gaza without a permit. Gazan college and university students also find it very difficult to move to and from the West Bank.

WHAT DOES "SECURITY" MEAN?

Security is generally defined as a "state of being free from threat." If this is the case, neither Israelis nor Palestinians are enjoying this state of being.

Israel does not accept that their occupation of the West Bank is illegal, and the Palestinians believe that they have the right to resist the illegal occupation. This is the heart of the issue.

Security is almost always used by Israel as the reason for the vast majority of their actions in the West Bank or Gaza. However, on the ground, in order to maintain its illegal occupation of the West Bank, Israel:

- acts like a sovereign power: controlling borders, determining policies, and writing the laws of the Occupied West Bank.

- withholds, whenever and for however long they decide, the taxes they collect every month on behalf of the Palestinian Authority.

- uses "administrative detention," summary house searches of those they perceive to be militants and protesters, and often uses lethal force against Palestinian youths who throw stones.

- continues to colonize the West Bank through illegal settlements and to provide soldiers to defend the settlers, as well as controlling around 500 checkpoints throughout the West Bank.

- is building the Separation Wall, the ultimate checkpoint.

The Palestinians also want security, and for them this involves the removal of the occupiers. Palestinians want the right to self-determination as individuals, communities, and as a sovereign nation, not occupation by Israel or any other nation. If the occupation were to end, all of the above restrictions on their lives would go, and so would their need for resistance.

The key problem is the crossover point where the two ill-matched parties clash. Israel has all the military, administrative, and economic power, which it wields systematically, while the Palestinians have very limited power, and their violence, including suicide bombings, is sporadic and specific to particular areas and times: flashpoints.

The lack of parity means that the Palestinians cannot win militarily (even if at times they feel compelled into violent conflict as their means of objecting to the harsh measures that Israel uses to maintain control). It is also increasingly clear that Israel cannot win by brute force. So Israel's security policies have not resulted in peace and security for either side.

As Desmond Tutu repeatedly reminds us: military force did not bring security to the white community in South Africa. Peace and justice did.

HOW ALL THIS AFFECTS PALESTINIANS TODAY

This is how Palestinians live under occupation. In the next part of the book you will read how Palestinian children and young people, from all over the West Bank, are directly affected by occupation. They will talk to you in their own voices about their pasts, their present, and the dreams they have for their futures and for their country.

Easter parade, Ramallah

RAMALLAH CITY AND THE QALANDIA CHECKPOINT

Ramallah is a Palestinian city in the central West Bank, about 6 miles, or 10 kilometers, north of Jerusalem. It has a population of about 27,000. Ramallah was historically a Christian town. Today Muslims form the majority of the population, but Christians still make up a significant minority.

The city itself sprawls over the crest of the Judean Hills and looks down on far-reaching, spare but beautiful valleys. Its position creates a comfortable climate. This city is also considered the cultural center of the West Bank and the most religiously diverse and tolerant part of Palestine.

Access to Ramallah from Jerusalem is via ten checkpoints, all staffed by Israeli security. None of these checkpoints are actually in Israel. Qalandia checkpoint is the main crossing in both directions. You cannot mention Ramallah without mentioning Qalandia. Controls are tight and people without the correct permits are not permitted to enter Jerusalem. Traffic going in either direction can be extremely slow.

The Qalandia Checkpoint

The village of Qalandia is dominated by the chaotic checkpoint. The roads are clogged with buses and trucks and the occasional cart. People selling drinks, SIM cards for cell phones, and other things lounge around on worn sofas. There is rubbish everywhere. Nobody loves this place. It is a wound, as is the Separation Wall, which looms brutally over everything. The noise, the fumes, and the desperation are palpable. Everybody

Street memorials for the dead, Ramallah

pushes, looking for advantage where there is none. Waiting and edging forward is all there is to do. The Israeli Defense Forces and other security take their time. They have shade. Identities are checked, vehicles and bags emptied and checked; arguments flare up and die down. The sense of powerlessness mixes in with the dust, chaos, and frustration.

These strictures are in place because of Israeli security fears. At this checkpoint the Palestinian and Israeli road networks meet. These roads link those from/into Ramallah with the road network of Jerusalem. This is where settler roads come together with ordinary access roads. The particular settler roads here connect the settlements with Israel through settler-checkpoints. Israeli Security considerations draw a noose around the free movement of Palestinians.

HOWARI BO MEDYAN SCHOOL, RAMALLAH

We get a taxi to take us to Howari Bo Medyan School, in Ramallah. It is in the busy, crowded, less privileged part of the Old City. It is early morning and the streets are lively with people shopping, going to work, street vendors shouting out prices, and the inevitable traffic chaos—buses competing with cars, motorbikes, and the pedestrians who spill onto the roads.

After many roadside discussions about the whereabouts of the school, we arrive. The children lining the stairs that lead to the front door greet us with smiles or curious looks. As we go up the stairs a bell sounds and all the children around us seem to be sucked into the building. Their day has begun.

The children we talked to were Muath, Mohammed,

The girls from the Howari Bo Medyan School

Kindah, Ibrahim, Basel, Tarteel, Abrar, Yara, and Sahed—five girls and four boys, aged 8 to 9 years old. The boys didn't want to be photographed, but we do have a photo of the five girls, plus one who didn't speak but wanted to be included.

WHERE THE CHILDREN ARE ORIGINALLY FROM

The towns or villages the children are originally from are: El Masra Sharqeya, Hebron, Nablus, Hebron—village of Samar, Mazare Nobani, Gaza Sheik, Zayed—central Gaza, Hebron—village of Seer, Tulkarem—Irtah, and Einqenya.

If you look at the map at the beginning of the book, you will see how dispersed Palestinians have become under occupation. This is the case for the whole West Bank: everybody is originally from somewhere else. Of the nine children, eight come from outside Ramallah.

What days do you like best?

Ibrahim: "Today is fun. School is fun."

Basel likes today: "Because you have come to visit us."

Another girl also likes today: "It's different, we have interesting classes and meeting you."

Basel: "I like Thursday best because I go back home to Tulkarem ... to aunts and uncles. We all go together as a family, to our land. We go home every Thursday and come back to Ramallah on Friday. I miss the land."

What is the trip home like?

Basel: "I'm mostly scared when there are settlers on the roads. They set up unofficial checkpoints along the road, wherever they like, and often fire at Palestinian people."

Does this happen often? Has it happened recently?

Basel: "Last Friday when we went back, settlers starting firing live bullets at the cars. Just to scare us."

Tarteel: "Our family used to live in Hebron. Sometimes going home to visit, soldiers made 'war' near the school. They do training—it's very scary. There are settlements close to Hebron and that's why the soldiers were there."

Mohammed: "Near Hebron and around the mountains there are Israeli settlements. We can't visit or play near the mountains because the settlers actually fire at children."

Kindah: "Once, when coming down the road to Nablus, from visiting family, settlers were shooting tear gas at people in cars. Some Palestinians threw stones back. I was with my mother and father. I was really scared. We were in a bus and we were made to get off, searched, and then got on the bus again, and searched again on the bus."

Mutah: "Once we were going back to our family's home village near Hebron. Settlers were shooting tear gas. We children went under the seats. The settlers searched the car. Soldiers were searching my grandfather's house nearby—there were stone throwers around—but the soldiers pick any houses to search."

Basel: "Once, while we were still living in Tulkarem, we saw three jeeps—one white, two black, and tanks. Tanks are scary."

Shahed: "One time, going to visit family in Hebron, soldiers stopped and searched the bus for a long time, and then made the bus turn back, even though they hadn't found anything. They just can."

Yara: "I am from Gaza, but our family is not allowed to return. The Israelis won't give us permits. My father lived in Ramallah before, so the family came here, but now we are stuck."

How often do these things happen?
Yara: "... Often ... all the time. Every Thursday or whenever we leave Ramallah."

What makes you happy?
Muath: "I like swimming and football,* but we can't get to the sea so I swim in the pool."

Basel: "I like swimming, football, and basketball, and want to do well at school."

Yara: "I like school, I also want to do well at school."

Kindah: "I want to go back to our original, unoccupied, country. It is my dream."

Shahed: "I like to be in the school play arranged by the teachers."

Abrar: "I want my parents always to be satisfied and happy with me."

*Football, for these children and teenagers, is what Americans call soccer. It is a popular free-time sport of both boys and girls in Palestine, as all it requires is a ball of some sort, a space to kick it about, and some makeshift goal posts ... tin cans, t-shirts, school bags, anything will do. And like kids in many other countries, they often support famous foreign sides like Real Madrid, Barcelona, Chelsea, Liverpool, or Manchester United, and hero-worship famous players like Messi and Ronaldo.

Tarteel: "I want my parents to be always happy with me. I want to be good at school."

Ibrahim: "I like swimming and football. I want to become a famous player for Barcelona."

Mohammed: "I wish Palestine would be free one day so we can live in peace and security."

Yara: "I want Palestine to be free, and I want to go back to Gaza with no checkpoints."

Basel: "I want to pass all my grades, and I would like Israel to be no more so that I could swim in the sea."

Yara: "I want to be successful and to become a doctor."

Ibrahim: "I want Jerusalem to be an open city for us, so I can be there and pray in my own city."

How do you see your future?
Mohammed: "I want to be a policeman. I want to protect Palestine."

Ibrahim: "I want to become a sheikh and pray for our people."

Tarteer: "I want to be a teacher and live in Hebron. I want to teach children to read and write, to eliminate illiteracy, and get children to enjoy sports ... physical education."

Abran: "I want to be a teacher so I can teach people how to defend their country."

Shabeh: "I want to be a doctor so I can help people in pain and find the best ways to treat sickness."

Muath: "I want to be a construction worker, so I can build my own house when I get married. They are too expensive in Ramallah."

Basel: "I want to be an architect, so I can build houses for poor people."

All the children love reading and tell us about their favorite stories and books.

These are the first children interviewed. They are also the youngest, but already clearly feeling the strain of occupied life, even from the relative security of Ramallah, a fairly safe place. However, moving away from Ramallah, into less safe places, the children's attitudes change, harden against the occupiers. It also becomes apparent that no matter where the children are, the older they get, the angrier they become, the more intractable and politicized.

THE TAMER INSTITUTE, RAMALLAH

The Tamer Institute for Community Education is a non-governmental organization (NGO) established in 1989. It was set up to meet the urgent needs of the Palestinian community during the First Intifada (uprising), 1987–1991. They saw that the most important of these needs was to acquire the means to help people learn and to express themselves in a difficult environment. Tamer works across the whole of the West Bank and Gaza Strip.

Palestine is a many-faceted place and not all of it is easily accessible. Tamer was our point of contact. Their tireless support made this project possible. They gave us introductions to important sources inside the Palestinian community, much-needed logistic support, advice, and—most importantly—kindness and goodwill around common ground, giving a voice to Palestinian children.

Tamer in Ramallah is a welcoming place, off a busy side street. There are books and pamphlets available, cheerful staff, and plenty of space for activities, quiet or otherwise. The children seem to have relaxed access to everything.

Two girls

Two girls—Shahad, age 8, and Aya, age 12—were keen to talk, although they didn't want their photos taken.

Aya: "My family are originally from Hebron. I am too young to remember why we came here. My dad works as a janitor for the Municipality and he makes food at home too, to sell on the street."

Shahad: "We are also originally from Hebron. My dad is an archaeologist."

Entrance to Tamer

Wall mural near Tamer

Do you like reading?
Aya: "No, not much."

Shahad: "I love reading."

What do you like to do that is interesting for you, or creative?
Aya: "I love drawing and painting. I want to be an illustrator and a painter. I also make things with beads."

Shahad: "I like playing football."

What's a normal day for you?
Aya: "Tamer is normal for us. We come every day, between 2 and 5. We can watch films and ..."

Shahad: "... and we can make things if we want ..."

What things are important for you in life?
Aya: "Respect, order, self-expression ..."

Shahad: "... health ..."

Tell me what a normal day for you is like.
Aya: "We go to school every day. Wear uniforms. School is normally from 8 till 12 or 1. Today we are early. I go to school on foot ..."

Shahad: "... I go by bus or in the car. I love school ..."

Aya: "... me too."

What do you like best at school?
Shahad: "I like English best, then Maths and Arabic ..."

Aya: "... I like Maths, Science, Arabic, and Art best."

What makes you happy?
Shahad: "Weddings and family occasions. I like going to my aunt's house for parties ... when I see my cousins and uncle too."

Aya: "Birthday parties when we go home to Hebron, and weddings."

How often do you go back to Hebron?
Aya: "For vacations. My sister lives there."

Shahad: "About once a month."

Are there any difficulties on your way there and back?
Shahad: "Sometimes there are soldiers, roadblocks, and that's always frightening, but mostly it's okay."

What makes you unhappy?
Aya: "When I remember my grandfather. He loved me very much. One day he left the house and just died."

ALICE, A TAMER MEMBER OF STAFF:
"Many of the children who come here after school are from very disadvantaged families. They go to school in the Old City, where people tend to be quite poor. A lot of their fathers are in Israeli political detention. As a result, a lot of them drop out of school to work in markets and places like that to help support the family. Uncles traditionally help support families with fathers in jail. Many children who come here are not originally from Ramallah. They tend to go home, as the girls were saying, for family occasions. They also go back in November to help with the olive harvest and also in the summer. These are big family events. The land is a big part of many of these families' lives. That's why many Palestinians speak of this occupation as the theft of their land.

Shahad: "When I remember my uncle. He died on a construction site. He had an accident. It's sad, because he was working hard in construction. The money is good. It's really sad because my cousins are without a father."

Three more young people

Three others have asked to be involved in the interviews. They are slightly older. Two young men, Massad, 17, and Muath, 20. They didn't want their photos taken. As soon as he sat down, Muath explained, "We don't know who'll see them [the photos] or who'll read what we say." They were later joined by Rand, a young woman of 15.

Muath: "I have been coming here since I was 16. I now work as a volunteer, supervising one of the teams doing Drama and Arts."

Massad: "I am also a Tamer volunteer and on Muath's team."

What do you do in your team?

Muath: "We work with mainly teenagers, from 13- to 20-years-old, on Saturdays and Tuesdays, from 3 o'clock for two to two and a half hours. It's all about the Arts here ... all kinds. We are now looking at acting as a way of expression ... through Drama.

I'm a student at Al Quds University in Ain Musbah, studying English literature."

Massad: "At the moment it's about rebuilding the team. New people come, old ones drop out. We get to know them all. We try and befriend people outside Tamer and bring them in here ... we try and give them some structure."

Muath: "... I joined this group in 2011. We did a Chekov play ... we weren't even told the title. We worked for nine months and performed for forty-five minutes. We called it *The Broken Window*. It was worth every minute, every minute. Nine months and one to two hours a week. It was fantastic. Our goals are to improve our skills."

What were your goals, Massad?

Massad: "I didn't know at the beginning. It just looked interesting, something new, but as we went on I wanted to 'say something' about myself, about our lives here in Palestine, as teenagers without a lot of hope. It helped me."

How do you mean, "without a lot of hope?"

Massad: "We are occupied. Do you know what that means? We cannot breathe without the Israelis' permission. They are everywhere. We are bound and gagged

... and it's getting worse. I want to study Drama at the Al Kasaba Theatre and Drama Academy. We'll see."

What about your families?

Massad: "My father is in prison. He is a political prisoner in Remon. We are allowed to visit once a year. He has been in for seven years and will be released in 2023. My mother is a housewife. I have two brothers and a younger sister."

Muath: "My family is tough. They refused to let me go to Canada, to study ... to escape from here. If I could, I would leave for Canada tomorrow. I spent three months there when I was 14. I really liked it."

Would you leave if you could?

Massad: "No. I want to stay. This is where I belong. My friends are here, my family. I want to work for Palestine's future ... through the Arts. We'll see."

Rand now joins the group. She also doesn't wish to have her photo taken.

Tell us something about yourself.

Rand: "I'm in the ninth grade at school and am thinking of becoming a fashion designer. I want to study abroad and leave Palestine. We are originally from Jerusalem, but moved to Ramallah for my father's job. My father and I are not allowed to return to Jerusalem, but my mother is. She's a teacher and also writes books for children. My father is Director of the A.M. Quattan Foundation* in Ramallah.

"I've only been to one meeting of my group. We're starting with drama activities ... getting to know each other. I will write in this group I hope."

What's your goal here, in the group?

Rand: "I want to change a bit, develop, do something with my time. My father is a Drama teacher. We like the Arts in our family."

What's a normal day for you?

Muath: "There are no normal days for a Palestinian. For us, the abnormal has become normal. However, I get up, come to the Tamer, eat and have coffee with friends ... play chess and video games. I like to be around friends."

Named after Abdel Mohsin Al-Qattan, a successful Palestinian businessman and advocate of Palestinian rights. The foundation was launched in London in 1994. It has become fully active in Palestine, offering and coordinating a range of cultural and educational projects focusing on Palestinian issues.

What makes your day not normal?
Muath: "It's not normal to be a prisoner in your own country, to not be able to move around freely and to have the opportunity to leave denied you by your family."

Rand: "Most days are normal for me. I go to school, play basketball, go home, and now I come to Tamer. It's okay. I suppose it's not normal to be locked out of your home city. I'm trying to move to Jerusalem, trying to get ID like my mother. There is not much hope."

Massad: "Normal for me is waking up, going to school, home for lunch, watching TV, opening my books, and studying. Normal. I don't have problems living in Ramallah. Not being able to visit my father is normal for me. When we do visit, once a year, it takes all day, with lots of waiting and checks and then we get very little time with him. We speak through a telephone, as he is separated by a glass screen. It's not good, but that is what they give us."

What makes you happy?
Rand: "Basketball, music, particularly Reggae ... our weather."

Muath: "Being with friends, people I love."

Massad: "Acting, listening to music, meeting friends, and drawing."

What makes you sad or angry?
Rand: "When people are rude and when there is too much pressure at school and the fact that our country is occupied by people who hate us."

Muath: "My family, and when there is religious fighting with my family. I meet people who are perfect at lying ... and I hate them for this. Why are they like that?"

Massad: "My father sometimes makes me sad ... and angry. Studying makes me angry. What's it for. It's for nothing. I won't need it in my future. I also hate angry people who shout."

Rand: "Some people outside Palestine don't understand what it's like here. We are hemmed in, prisoners. This does not make the future look easy or normal. We don't know what normal is ..."

Muath: "Yeah, the world thinks of Palestinians as terrorists. We are just people trying to live here. Living in a prison, with no freedom of movement. We have to ask permission, we need ID."

How do you see your future and that of your country?

Rand: "I want peace. One state. Will it happen? I don't think so."

Muath: "There was hope for change on several occasions, but now we have sunk into apathy. We are fighting ourselves. We are doing the Israelis' work for them. We are losing the will to fight. At Nakba Day* this year there were only fifteen people and they were just singing and dancing. It is no longer political."

Massad: "I want to be mayor one day. I would fix the streets, plant trees. Make it perfect."

Do you think you can do anything about the situation?

Rand: "Palestinians have to change the way they think. Their everyday lives are a joke now. People have stopped talking about the situation, sharing knowledge about their lives and their people. Only Palestinians can change things and make a difference. If we believe Palestine can be free, it can, but without the belief, without the hope,

*Nabka means catastrophe in Arabic. This day, May 15, is when Palestinians remember the catastrophe for them that was the establishment of the State of Israel (1948).

there can be no change. My grandmothers were 15 and 20 at Nakba. It's being lost. Our loss is being forgotten."

Another visit to Tamer

On another day, Mohammad wants to talk to us.
Mohammad: "I am 17 years old. I come from here, from Ramallah. Our family village is Sair, Hebron. My dad is an accountant and he coaches karate a bit. He was a champion once. My mom is a housewife.

"My dad has been in Israeli prisons five times, for six years altogether. He used to stand up to Israeli soldiers. Once, a soldier pushed my dad's grandmother. What could he do? Another time Israeli soldiers gathered all the people of Tahta, our neighborhood ... they were searching for someone, and a soldier slapped my father. So he slapped the soldier back. But you cannot defend yourself against Israeli soldiers.

"My dad went to prison when I was 8. He had been three times already before I was born. It was hard for my mother. I was 10 when he went in again. He went in for two years that time. It's tough."

How did it make you feel?

"I am proud of him. And it makes me feel angry with the Israelis. The family stayed strong. We got community support. I worked in the market before school and that helped a little. My mom worked a bit too. I am the oldest. I have two brothers and a sister. We are a strong family."

What do you want from your life when you finish school?

"I want to study journalism and to be a poet. I write poems."

What is life like now your father is out of prison?

"Much better. Not so many problems. My father cannot leave Palestine now. It's forbidden. But this is the same for many Palestinians. We are locked in here, cut off from the world."

What are the main difficulties in your life?

"When they arrested my father the second time—he was the leader of a political group; he represented Hamas at a college—the soldiers pointed their guns at me. I was 10. I was terrified. I will never forget that.

"My father is no longer a leader. He stopped that. So, life is easier."

What makes your parents unhappy now?

"My youngest brother doesn't know his father well. He used to sleep with Mom when Dad was in prison. He doesn't like Father back in her bed. When he first came back my brother was always asking, 'Who is he?' but it's slowly getting better.

"And you know, my father asked to go on a Haj* to Jerusalem, but the Israelis denied that. None of us are allowed to visit Jerusalem.

"I went once, in the trunk of a car with friends who are allowed. I just wanted to see Jerusalem.

"... I hate seeing the Wall. It's wrong. It shouldn't be there. We are in our country and the Israelis draw a line, many lines actually, and say we are forbidden to go places or we need passes ... in our own country. Those who built this wall do not own the land, so how is it possible for them to do this?

"But the people in Gaza are much worse off ... so I don't know."

*Haj refers to a religious pilgrimage.

Mohammad asks us: "What do you think of the situation in Palestine?"

We responded that, for the sake of the book we "did not think anything." However, we did point out that we were here to give the world a window onto the lives of Palestinian children and young people, and their families, living in very difficult situations, living under occupation.

Mohammad: "It isn't normal that many Palestinian children lose parents and have to struggle. I want you to show this in your book. Why don't the British people help us? And why did they give Palestine to the Zionists?"

We said that not enough people know about the situation and that this most of all, is why we are here ... to show aspects of their story, so often untold.

Mohammad: "We have given up our heritage. We have left our tradition behind. How can things change if we forget who we are? Look at the Separation Wall, our politics. Where is our future, our strategy? In Palestine, people can't control the government. Our government is not good. It's corrupt and obeys orders from stronger countries. It takes money from America in return for 'good behavior.'"

What three things would you change?

"The world would become one ... no divisions. And Jewish people should go where they belong. Russians in Russia, Germans in Germany. The original Jewish population of Israel, about 6%, can stay and live here with no problems, but the others are not wanted ... and any Jewish person that stays must teach their children that they are not the best people, not God's people. We are all the same under God. The same."

JENIN

Jenin is a city at the northernmost reaches of the West Bank, with a population of around 40,000. It lies on the edge of a rich agricultural plain, making it a major agricultural center for the surrounding towns. The city serves as the administrative center of the Jenin Governorate, and is under the administration of the Palestinian Authority.

Jenin's position in the West Bank is unique in a way. One factor is its distance from major urban centers and from the Separation Wall. Another is that nowadays there is less pressure from Israeli troops or settlers—they have drawn back from this area. Most of the refugees living here came from Haifa in the Nakba of 1947–48. During the First Intifada (1987–1991), Jenin was known as a center of the resistance, and the refugee camp here (Balata) came under fierce Israeli attack. But now life in Jenin is as normal as it can be under occupation.

However, violence is still not far away. The Director of the Freedom Theater in Jenin, Juliano Mer-Khamis, was killed by masked gunmen in the city in April of 2011. Mer-Khamis had co-founded the theater with Zakaria Zubeidi, former military chief of the al-Aqsa Brigades (a loose-knit group of Palestinian armed groups, fighting the occupation). Both Mer-Khamis and Zubeidi had renounced violence as a solution to the occupation of Palestine.

ANIMATION WORKSHOP IN THE OLD JENIN LIBRARY

We are in the old Jenin Library to talk to local young people who are here to take part in an animation workshop, run by two UK volunteers, Gary and Jan. This building was once a palace belonging to the leader of a local clan in the Ottoman period. It is now the Sharek Cultural Center for local youth. Sharek means "engage." It is the ambition of the local municipality to renovate the thirteen buildings like this one in the area, for the development of tourism.

Jenin wall art; and Jenin Freedom Theatre

Animation workshop in Old Jenin Library

We meet Ahmad (the local Tamer coordinator), the local volunteers, and "The Palm Tree" team—a group of 13- to 14-year-olds who read and discuss books. All the boys here are from outside villages, and the girls are from Jenin itself. The boys have no animation experience; the girls have some and have also made a short film.

First we talk to Gary, one of the visiting animators.

Gary: *"You have to draw in a way that you can show children that they can do it themselves. I demonstrate to the children and they then follow. They continue in this way with me showing, letting them draw and me actively monitoring. The idea is to concentrate on the process. Showing them how to do something, express themselves as simply as possible. In this way, when they come to create an animation storyboard they can achieve this simply and effectively."*

Abdel Aziz and Yasmeen
The children, who are keen to be interviewed, come to another part of the room. They introduce themselves. (Yasmeen is not her real name, to protect her family.)

Abdel Aziz: "I am 16, in the tenth grade at school. My dad is a merchant and my mother is a hairdresser."

Yasmeen: "I am 14, in the ninth grade."

Abdel Aziz: "My father came from Nouris,

Abdel Aziz

a '1948' village, one that was taken over by the Israelis. They demolished it and everybody was forced into the Jenin Camp. That's what happened a lot in 1948. My mom was also from a village near Jenin, but she escaped to Jordan. A lot of people did then. It was safer for them there. They were more welcome than in their own country.

"My parents met at his brother's wedding in Amman, Jordan. Mom was the sister of the bride. It's a nice story. They came to live in the Jenin Camp. We left the camp after the Second Intifada (2000–2005). It was too dangerous and we moved to Fakoua, just outside Jenin, where my mother originally came from."

Yasmeen: "Both my parents are from Yamoun, a village near Jenin. It was an arranged

Yasmeen

marriage. They didn't see each other until the wedding day ... and we still live there."

Do you like school?

Abdel Aziz: "Yes. I get high grades. I want to be a doctor. I really want to study abroad, because it's difficult here. There is more support abroad, more scholarships and stuff."

Yasmeen: "I want to be in the media. To tell people what happens in life, particularly here, to our people and our land. I would love to be a journalist. It would be exciting and sometimes dangerous. But my parents think the only suitable job for a woman is teaching. Yes, I like school, but I like time off too."

Abdel Aziz: "School is a journey for me. I feel I am doing something important."

Yasmeen: "I like reading. I'm always reading. I've read *Gone with the Wind*, Victor Hugo's *Les Miserables*, many Palestinian novels."

Abdel Aziz: "I prefer reading political works and history. But I will write when there is a competition. I like writing."

What's a normal day for you like?

Yasmeen: "School, reading, watching TV, and listening to music ... and I write poetry and stories sometimes, but I'm never happy with my stories. They are hard to write."

Abdel Aziz: "I am happiest when all the members of my family are together. I have an older brother in Israel, so it doesn't happen all the time. I am unhappy when there is stress in the family. My father has money worries. He had a currency exchange business, but he was robbed. It is sometimes difficult about money.

"If everything is okay, I like to read the Koran and come to community things like this. I like being involved in my community. I do a lot of chatting on Facebook too. I also like making things out of wood, models and things."

Can you tell me more about your families?

Abdel Aziz: "I have three brothers and a sister. Two of my brothers are older ..."

Yasmeen: "I have seven brothers and two sisters. I am the younger girl and one brother is younger. Two of my brothers are in Israeli prisons. The older one, he is 20, was accused of supporting a boy who killed an Israeli soldier. He has a twenty year sentence.

"The other brother, who was 16 then, had a toy revolver. He took it to a friend's to show them. Then another boy told the Israelis. They came and searched our house and found the toy gun. He was convicted because he was the brother of a convicted man ... our other brother ... and sentenced to eight years. The soldiers, when they came looking for the gun, tore our house up. They were convinced we were a terrorist family, but it was a toy gun.

"The younger one will be released in a month. The other one has twelve years to serve. We last visited them five months ago."

Abdel Aziz: "My father spent twenty days in prison too. He wrote bad checks when we didn't have any money."

What makes life difficult for you?

Abel Aziz: "When soldiers come to Fakoua or around our area. We all feel unsafe and in danger. They can do what they like 'for Israeli security.' Recently, they've been around every day. Everybody gets scared. They lie and say we throw stones over the Separation Wall at them."

Yasmeen: "Life can be difficult with brothers in prison. Our father is sick and can't work. He used to go and work in Israel without a permit. But the Israelis caught him and beat him badly. He has only limited movement now. My other brothers—who are 24, 26, and 27—all work in Israel. They don't have permits either, but they get smuggled into Israel. There are gaps in the Wall. The Israelis put them there so cheap labor can come in ...

"Our father is at home all day and this is not good in our culture. He feels bad, but what can he do? He likes the garden, thank God ... he at least has something ... but our economic situation makes him crazy and sad. It is difficult."

How do you see your own future and that of Palestine?

Abdel Aziz: "I think war is approaching for Palestine ... with Israel ... I want to be a doctor, but looking at my country's political conditions ... I just don't know.

"Apart from that, I would like to use multimedia to share ideas. I would also like to do something to help people in need ... especially for young children who have to work, and the elderly."

What three things would you change?

Yasmeen: "I would make more services and public things. Take them away from the private. Then things could be run for the people, not as businesses. I would also look at changing some of our traditions ... ones that are so biased against women. I would give women more freedom of choice in their lives. Now we are 'protected' all the time from life, from decisions and taking part in many things.

"I would also like to see the law against children working properly enforced and finally, that we could study whatever we want, not be forced to study what others decide is 'good for us.'"

Abdel Aziz: "I want the Israelis to go back to their countries. Local Jewish Palestinian people can stay. They belong here too. You know, the Palestinian Authority recognized Israel out of despair to end the occupation. It hasn't worked.

"I would also change the economic conditions of the whole country. I would make us more developed and modern. Development is badly needed.

"And lastly, I want more respect for myself. I want to be in a position in the community that demands respect. I can do this if I become the Mayor. If I do the job well I will get respect. I don't want respect to come just from the position."

And when we had finished, Abdel Aziz said to us:

"And I would like to see what you write … when the book is ready. Okay?"

We agreed.

Nablus is a city in the very northern reaches of the West Bank. It is about 30 miles or 49 kilometers north of Jerusalem. The population is roughly 130,000. Nablus is the capital of the Nablus Governorate and a Palestinian commercial and cultural center.

Today, the population is predominantly Muslim, with small Christian and Samaritan minorities. Since 1995, the city has been governed by the Palestinian National Authority.

Nablus has always been noted for its fierce independence and opposition to outside interference in its affairs.

A WALK IN THE OLD CITY

The labyrinthine Old City lanes snake upwards and finally lead us into bright sunlight and onto a plateau-like square ... Al Qaryon—it has its place in the story, as well as the history of this conflict.

On looks and feel alone, it could be any number of places in the historic Mediterranean, but it is not. What marks this square out is the proliferation of plaques hammered onto or otherwise affixed to the ancient, rampart-type walls that rise above the square, atop which sit houses. These plaques are the punctuation marks in the city's history. This square is the heart of the city, which in itself is the heart of yet another story in this conflict.

Today it is a friendly space, bright and warm in the afternoon sun.

A shopkeeper here relates this story. He didn't want to give his name. We will call him Mohammad.

What are all the plaques about? Some have photos ...
Mohammad: "The plaques are memorials to those who died in 2002, when Israeli soldiers invaded."

Why did they invade?
"It was the second uprising, the Intifada ... we were fighting them."

He points up to a position above the square where there is a woman hanging out washing in her courtyard.

"... Up there. A tank came over the top of a house, bulldozed a family home. The whole family were inside. A pregnant woman, her husband, grandfather and children—all killed by the tank. They were not fighters.

"My shop, not this one, the one over there, had a public phone outside it in those days. The Israeli soldiers wired it up with dynamite. It blew up and killed the first person who used it."

How are things now?

"They still come a lot, sometimes daily, and take away people for questioning. It's just to intimidate us. They tell the world we are monsters and terrorists, but we are not."

What do the Israelis want from all of this?

"They want all the land. They want us to leave. But where would we go? To Jordan, Syria? No, this is our home ... my home. What can we do? They control us."

An apartment in Nablus

Next day we go to a prearranged meeting with Reyad Habash, a teacher here in Nablus, and his wife Samah, a nurse. Reyad has asked two boys from Balata Camp to come to his apartment and speak to us. No photos of the apartment are available.

Reyad and Samah have been married for four years and have two children. Jana, their daughter, is 3, and Mohammad, their son, is 19 months. Their parents help look after the children as they both work.

BALATA CAMP

Balata Camp is adjacent to the city of Nablus. It is the largest refugee camp in the West Bank. Today, the camp is very densely populated, with 30,000 residents in an area of just under one-tenth of a square mile, or 0.25 square kilometers. Extreme overcrowding, unemployment, and poverty bring tensions and health issues, mental as well as physical.

This Palestinian refugee camp was first suggested by the United Nations in 1948 and finally accepted by the displaced refugees in 1950, when they saw they had little choice. At that time, the camp was considered temporary; until 1956, the residents lived in tents. Yet the third generation of those originally displaced are still living there, denied access to Jaffa (Yaffa) which was once, for the majority, their home.

Reyad's father is originally from Yaffa (Jaffa) and is a retired teacher.

Two boys from Balata

First we meet Qais.

Qais: "I am 10 years old. I have two sisters and five brothers. I am in the middle. I go to school in the camp. I am in grade four. We all live in Balata. My family are originally from Yaffa, but my parents were also born in the camp. My grandfather was born in Yaffa. My father is a policeman. My mother stays at home."

What do you like to do in your free time?
"I like to study. I like school. I want to become a teacher at university. I want to teach people to be good in their lives. To teach students to become doctors to help suffering patients."

What makes you happy?
"Playing with my friends. I have some friends. We enjoy playing football. My best friend is called Ahmad. I also like eating *mansaf* (chicken and rice). It's my favorite."

What is a good day for you?
"Friday is a great day. I play football all day. My brothers and other family go to the mosque together. I prefer to pray at home."

What's a bad day for you?
"Saturdays are not so good. My friends usually come over and ask me to play football. But I refuse. I want to study. They sometimes hit me, hurt me, because I don't want to play. I have a laptop at home, so I can play computer games when I have a break from study."

What makes your family unhappy?
"We always have money problems. My father's salary is not enough for us."

Have you had any problems with the Israeli soldiers?
"I get frightened sometimes. It's when the Israelis come once a week to pray at the Tomb of Jusef (Joseph). The soldiers come with them, for security they say, and they shoot in the air. They just look threatening and unfriendly. Also, they can just arrest you ... My father was arrested ten years ago. He was in prison for four to five years, for political reasons—during the first Intifada, in 1987. A long time ago."

We next meet Hamad. He is also from the camp. He is a distant cousin of Reyad's.

Hamad: "I am 12 years old. I have four brothers and three sisters. My father works for Nablus Municipality. My mother stays at home. My family are originally from Yaffa."

Do you like life here?
"No, not really. I don't want to live in Balata forever. I want to live outside in Nablus somewhere. A normal place."

Why ... What's wrong with Balata?
"People hurt each other there, they fight. It's too crowded—30,000 people live in a very small area."

What do people fight about?

"It usually starts between children then parents interfere. It's crowded and tense all the time."

Is it difficult to leave the camp? To live outside?

"Yes. You need money and there are no opportunities for jobs."

Have you visited anywhere outside the camp?

"Yes. I've been to Nablus, of course, and Qalqilya, Jericho, and to Tel Aviv. My father has a permit to visit Israel."

Tell me about your life.

"I've left school already. I help my father in the market. He is a trader when not working for the Municipality. I left school after grade six. I didn't want to waste any more time."

What else would you change about your life?

Hamad: "Our house is too small. We all live in one room—nine people. I would also get rid of Israeli guns in our lives. They come into Balata every day and make a lot of noise and trouble. They come in cars and sometimes in tanks and they often arrest people. We all stay inside when this happens. We are terrified. My father is a peaceful man. He's never been arrested.

"I would like to open a shop one day with my father. My parents sell socks in the market after my father finishes work at lunchtime."

Reyad: "Sometimes youths go to Jusef's tomb when the Israeli settlers come to pray and they throw stones in protest. Hamad doesn't. The soldiers fire in the air when the kids throw stones. Hamad gets terrified by gunfire. You know, there are usually four soldiers to every settler at the tomb. There are many settlements near Nablus. It is always tense here; never ending."

QATTANA

The village of Qattana

Qattana is a small, prosperous Palestinian village, 7.5 miles or 12 kilometers northwest of Jerusalem. The population is around 750. The village is surrounded by the Palestinian villages of Qibya and Beit 'Anan in the north, the illegal Israeli settlement of Har Adar in the south, the Israeli Separation Wall in the south and the west, and by Biddu village to the east.

The Wall cuts many off from their land, limits movement, and sometimes denies people free access to family and basic services: schools, hospitals, transportation, and welfare. Even the water supply to the village is controlled from the Israeli side of the Wall.

THE HOUSE BEHIND THE WALL: A SPECIAL CASE

The house belongs to Najem El-Din Taher Al-Husseini, an elderly Palestinian man. He is the grandfather of the two boys we have come to talk to. He is head of the family. The house is adjacent to the Israeli settlement of Har Adar, which was built in 1986 on Qattana land. The house is located on the eastern edge of Qattana and sits in a no man's land between the Wall and the village. Access to and from the house is controlled by Israeli security via an electronically controlled gate. It is neither in Qattana village nor in Israeli territory.

It is a house that is "nowhere." The full weight of the occupation bears down on the family every day.

These are the facts. Below are the voices of the people who live there, although "survive" would probably be a better word than "live."

There are eighteen family members living in this 1,550-square-foot, or 144-square-meter, house. The house has four rooms, a kitchen, and a bathroom. The family has no free access to the village and depends on Israeli soldiers to open the gates for them. Nobody except family members can enter through these gates. Their water supply has also been cut and water is delivered only every two weeks by tanker, from which the family fill drums. And the phone line has been cut. In effect, the family has no access to Palestinian or Israeli services. Their situation gives real meaning to the term "no man's land."

This situation is having serious negative effects on the family, especially on the two teenage boys.

How did this situation come about?

After the Israeli military order of December 2003 (see the side bar), the family were given a choice. It was this: move away and lose their land to the Wall, or stay, cut off, behind the Wall. They chose to stay on their land.

Our purpose in visiting Qattana is to talk to the two teenage boys who live in the house "behind the gate."

THE CONSEQUENCES OF THE SEPARATION WALL FOR QATTANA

On December 9, 2003, the Israeli forces handed the residents of Qattana a military order (number 84/03/T) to confiscate 47 acres or 192,000 square meters of land from their village, as well as from the nearby village of Al Qubeiba. This was done so Israel could construct the Separation Wall. This cost the village 26 acres or 106,000 square meters of land, as this land fell inside the Wall. It became Israeli land. In addition, another military order (number 107/03/T) was issued by the Israeli occupation on December 31, 2003, to confiscate 59 acres or 238,000 square meters more land from Qattana, Biddu, Beit Surik, and Al Qubeiba villages. The Separation Wall in Qattana village reaches a length of 3.7 miles or 6 kilometers, isolating 47% of the village's total land. This land has now been lost.

This was done for Israeli "security" reasons.

The Israelis have given permission for the boys to come through the gate and talk to us.

What follows is an account of what happened and what is still happening to one family as a result of the building of this Wall.

Arrangements had been made. We walked up to the top of the hill, overlooking the village. There they were, on the other side of the wire mesh gates, with their grandfather, on their side of the fence. We had been given to understand that the boys would be allowed out to talk to us at the library in Qattana.

Almost immediately, an armored Israeli personnel carrier arrived on the other side of the gate. A soldier opened his door and stood on the running board. He shouted at us and waved us away. Our Tamer guide, Samar, translated and told us that permission for the boys, Hamzeh (14) and Basel (13), to meet us had been withdrawn. No reason was given. The boys would not be allowed out after all. It was made perfectly clear that our camera was also to be put away.

The soldier became increasingly agitated as we stood there, so we spoke as quickly as we could to the boys through the wire gate.

51

It was very tense.

What is most frightening about your situation?

Hamzeh: "The presence of the Israelis. They are everywhere. We cannot move about. When they come they are loud. They shout and scare us."

Basel: "They cause us problems getting to school. They are always slow to open the gates. They usually take half an hour to an hour to let us out, then the walk to school is then thirty minutes. So ..."

Hamzeh: "The main thing for us is freedom in our own village, in our own lives."

The soldier, having gone back into the vehicle, emerges again, and from the running board shouts at us and motions us to leave. He is more and more agitated. He is waving us away. We have no option but to leave.

BACK IN THE VILLAGE OF QATTANA

We go back down the hill and into Qattana and the village hall where Jan and Gary are conducting another illustration and animation workshop for the local children.

We talk to Samar, our facilitator in so much here, *and to a local volunteer, who wanted to remain anonymous.*

Volunteer: "The family have a permit to live near the wall, but there is no electricity or water. And they cannot build any more rooms. There are eighteen people in that house. So, in theory, the land has not been confiscated, but no one is really allowed to use it in a normal way. And it is their land. Now, according to Israeli military law, if the land is not cultivated after three years, the landowners lose their rights over the land.

"The Wall here is a mesh fence. So they can move it if they want and take more land in this way. People have been to the High Court to fight confiscation. Then the Israelis appeal. In the meantime, the situation stays the same. And many Palestinians won't go to the Israeli court. They are afraid or do not have the resources. People are 'keeping their heads down' more and more. We are losing everything in this way. Anyway, the court usually recognizes Israel's right to do this.

"Even our own Village Council doesn't help in this fight."

Samar: "The village is rich. The Council wants to avoid trouble with the Israelis.

It sometimes feels hopeless. And the Israeli settlements nearby are expanding, especially Har Adar. It was built eighteen years ago and is illegal, but the Israelis have got round that by saying it is part of Greater Jerusalem and therefore comes under stricter security constraints."

We are in the Council offices to speak to Aisha, the daughter-in-law of Najem El-Din Taher Al-Husseini, and the mother of the two boys, Basel and Hamzeh. She has suddenly been allowed out through the gates and can now do some much needed shopping for the family. As she says, "I never know when I will be allowed out or for how long. When they say I can, I go ... quickly."

Aisha: "My name is Aisha. I have six sons and one daughter. I have lived in this house for twenty years. My eldest son is 18 years old."

When was the Wall built?
"The big new gate was put up in 2003, so it was finished then. Before that, there was another smaller gate and we had a key. Now with the big, electronic gate we have no key."

How far is your land from the gates?
"It is all our land and goes back about 10 acres from the Wall to the house. But we can't cultivate it because we don't have any water."

How do you get your food?
"When we get allowed out we walk down the hill to the village. We get a taxi back to the gates and then use a horse and cart on the other side ... to get everything to the house that way."

Do the children have any problems because of the situation?
"My older son has back problems. This is caused by the long walk to school with a heavy bag. But all the young ones are unhappy and upset the whole time. This is not a natural, healthy situation for young people."

How are they doing at school?
"They all did well at first. Then they went downhill. They have a sense of hopelessness, of 'why bother.' They end up saying, 'I hate school.' It's very damaging to them."

Does this affect how they are at home?
"They are angry a lot. It takes them an hour to get home from school. When they get home they are angry. They usually throw their books away. They don't want to see the books."

Are your children getting any help with these problems?

"The UNRWA* for Palestine sends therapists. All the children need this help. But to send all the children to see the therapist would be too much for us to pay. We decided to help Mohammad. He is my 9-year-old son. He's in third grade. He is in most need of help. He is abusive at school. He's learning nothing ... not taking part. He is the brightest of my children. Najas, my eldest son, is 18 and is sitting exams. Until last year all his grades were good ... but this year, he has failed everything."

Where is the children's father today?

"He lives with us, but today he is visiting his sister. He has worked in construction, but he's not working now. Work is difficult to find. His father, who owns the land, doesn't work either. He has had open heart surgery."

How do you live then?

"We don't live ... we survive. We depend on the UNRWA who provide us with basic supplies every three months. They give us 30 shekels** per month each. However, recently they have cut our allowance in half. We make do. We have no gas for cooking. We cut down old trees. We also

had an organization in Jerusalem who adopted the family for a year, but now they are reconsidering."

Why did you decide to stay behind the Wall?

"We had no money to go elsewhere. This is our only land, our only livelihood. Grandfather could have sold the land to the Israelis, but we would have been considered traitors in the village. But now, the villagers think we are taking money from the Israelis ... to stay! We lose both ways."

Do you see a solution?

"I only went [up] to ninth grade at school. What can I do? But if I was head of the family I would stay, even though the stress on the whole family is so great. My husband is violent and needs treatment. There is treatment being offered, but it would be at 100 shekels a time, so he refuses to go. He should go for the children. If I argue about it with him he beats me. I think long term about his problems, but he only thinks day by day. His pain and frustration makes him violent. He tries, you know. Twice a week he takes all the family laundry to his sister's here in the village. He carries it on his head, then comes back and slumps

*The United Nations Relief and Work Agency for Palestine.

**Roughly equivalent to $8.

down outside the gate, exhausted. The men have to go outside for the toilet. There is no water for that. In winter, baths are okay for the children, but in the summer they need showers every day. I send them down to my father's house in the village."

What else has changed?

"We had two cars, but the Israelis took them. We were taking one of the children to hospital one night and they stopped us on the road. They said the registration had expired, so they confiscated the car. We then took the second car to the hospital and the same thing happened. We appealed, but lost. Even taxis we travel in can be stopped and fined, but so far it's been okay."

What about the two boys we saw, Hamzeh and Basel, what's the worst thing for them?

"The most disturbing thing for them is that they can't see their friends after school. The family won't let them out again to play football or join birthday parties or other celebrations.

"The family believes they will have problems getting back. Ahmed, my 15-year-old, is the worst with school. He goes out in the morning, but plays truant. When he's at home, he sits in front of the TV and won't talk to anyone."

What do Basel and Hamzeh want for their futures?

"Basel wants to be a carpenter and has asked to join a special school. Hamzeh wants to be an ironsmith. They need space. We all do. My husband and I live in one room with seven children. My brother-in-law and five children live in another, and the grandfather and grandmother live in another. My little girl, Ayana, lives with cousins during the week so she can go to kindergarten. She comes back at the weekends.

"We are being squeezed out by Israel, by the settlements. Nobody is stopping them. We lost out in the Oslo agreement. The Palestinian authority agreed to leave three settlements in the north, but they are just expanding and will overpower us. They even have a university there now. The Palestinian Authority does nothing. They cannot admit the mistakes of Oslo, so no one speaks about what is going on. That's what I think, anyway."

As she gets up to leave, she shows us a photograph. "This is all my children. I show you this so you recognize them."

This is a woman under siege, her house cut off, her family life increasingly unmanageable.

SEBASTIYA

Sebastiya is a Palestinian village of over 4,500 inhabitants in the West Bank, about 1.24 miles or 2 kilometers northwest of the city of Nablus. Much of the village lands (42%) are located in Area C under the Oslo Accords. In effect, this means that the village is surrounded by an Israeli presence. (See the introduction/pages 11 and 12 for a full explanation.)

In Sebastiya we talk to three girls: Lina, 10; Hadil, 10; Seema, 10; and a boy, Tala, who is 11.

Can you tell me a little about yourselves? Your families, your normal day ... things that make you happy?

Lina: "I am from Sebastiya. My father is from here and my mother is from a village near here. I have two sisters and two brothers. My father works in the Ministry of Education and my mother is a teacher.

"I get up early and go to school. I come back for lunch and I watch TV or play on the computer. I then play with my sister and some friends. We play hopscotch and hide and seek. I go on Facebook sometimes."

What makes you happy?

Lina: "Playing with friends makes me happiest and visiting relatives. And I love eating strawberries and wild berries."

Hadil: "I have one brother and two sisters. My dad is from Jordan. Sometimes he

Ancient site, Sabastiya

View of Israeli settlement from Sebastiya

works in restaurants or with electricity and my mom is from Sebastiya. She stays at home. Most days I get up and go to school too, then come home and study. If there are exams I study extra hard. In my free time I visit my grandmother here in Sebastiya. She tells me stories ... fantasy stories like 'Little Red Riding Hood' and the Arabic version of 'Leila and the Fox.' My mother once told me a story called 'Labneh' ('Cheese').

"I enjoy school a lot. English is my favorite subject. It's not too complicated, but not easy either. I want to be a doctor and English will help me.

"I am happiest when I succeed in exams, playing with my friends, watching funny cartoons ... Tom and Jerry are the best."

Seema: "My father is from Sebastiya and I don't know where my mother is from originally. On normal days I go to school and when I come home I do my homework. Then I play with friends, hide and seek, skipping. Sometimes I fight with my sister over clothes ...

"I love reading. Stories, magazines ... anything. My favorites are 'Little Red Riding Hood' and *I Will Never Not Ever Eat a Tomato*. I love talking to my parents and my sister."

Tala: "I have two brothers. My mother is from Nablus and my father from Sebastiya. My mother has an embroidery business and my father works as a blacksmith in Israel. I lived in Nablus for a while. I prefer it here.

I go to school and come home and do homework, then I go on the computer for an hour or so. I usually watch TV at about 3 PM. Or go on Facebook and talk to friends. I have eighty-five friends ... from Nablus, Syria, and Sebsatiya, and some are my relatives who don't live here, especially my grandmother and grandfather. My grandfather loves Facebook.

"The happiest day for me is my birthday."

Is there anything that makes you unhappy?
Seema: "Fighting with my sister sometimes over clothes."

Hadil: "When I get bad marks in school and when I fight with my sister. Those are not good things. I also hate it when we can't go to something because it's the boys' day ... like at the library. I can't just go when I want. It makes me really angry."

Is there anything that makes your parents unhappy?

Hadil: "When I go to our land and climb trees. They are afraid I will hurt myself. I am not afraid.

"They don't like it when Israeli soldiers come into town. They usually come after children have thrown rocks at them. Sometimes they fire their guns, just to scare us. Sometimes they arrest children."

Lina: "... they took my 14-year-old cousin away once, for two days. They brought him back in the middle of the night ... at 2 AM. They like to disturb us. All the families were angry and upset ..."

What did they want with him?

Lina: "We don't know. He doesn't tell anybody what happened."

Hadil: "When the soldiers come into the town, the boys sometimes throw rocks. Usually the girls don't. But we all get really frightened. They come in army cars with guns on them and they're scary."

When do they normally come?

Lina: "We never know when they're going to come. They just come, but they always come when there are Jewish holidays."

Tala: "My parents worry about our land. We all do. In 2006, the Israeli settlement closest to us, Shavi Shomron, put up a fence which cut off some of our land ..."

Seema: "... the village tore it down. It was illegal. Then sometime in 2012 they started flooding our land with sewage from pipes in the settlement. When we discovered it we protested. Soldiers came with noise bombs and gas. Some people were hurt."

What happened?

Lina: "We got help. We were lucky. Some British tourists came here and they heard about the sewage. I don't know exactly what happened, but they went back to the UK and told somebody. It got mentioned in Parliament ... I don't know ... but it stopped. We were lucky. We are twinned* with somewhere in the UK because of this."

What three things would you like to change if you could?

Hadil: "I want to travel to other places, like France, and live in a big house like a palace. Or live in Germany, in a big house

*Twinning refers to two towns in different places having a special agreement to be Twin Towns. This relationship is designed to promote peace, friendship, and understanding, as well as trade and tourism.

by the sea. We can't go to the sea. We can't get permits."

They all agree, they would love to see the sea.

Tala: "We went to the Dead Sea once, when I was very young. We rented a house. It was nice, but it's too hard to get permission now."

All the families seem to have land outside the village, as is the Palestinian custom. The children all agree that the best time of the year is the harvest, when everybody goes to the land and helps out. They have olive, lemon, cherry, apricot, and almond trees and also grow tomatoes, peppers, pomegranates, and vine leaves. They agree, "It's the best ..."

AHMED, LOCAL FARMER AND VOLUNTEER

After talking to the children we meet Ahmed Khaled, a local farmer and volunteer. He is also active in the Twinning Association. He knows the history of the village and talks freely. At the top of a hill, above the village, he stops and opens his arms wide.

Ahmed: "The ancient site of Samaria-Sebaste is located here. The ruins are all around the hillside and are the remains from six cultures dating back 10,000 years:

Canaanite, Israelite, Hellenistic, Herodian, Roman, and Byzantine. We are very old here, very old."

Do you get a lot of tourists here?
Ahmed: "We used to. So many ... the streets would be stuck with tour buses. They were mostly sent by Israeli travel firms. It was at its peak round 1999, I think."

What happened to them?
Ahmed: "Slowly, slowly, the increase in Israeli checkpoints, barriers, and restricted roads made it too difficult to get here. The village is getting poorer because of this."

We walk a little farther and come to a stop on a precipice, overlooking a valley. A small, modern-looking settlement is visible in the middle distance.

What's that village there?
Ahmed: "That's Shavi Shormon. It's an Israeli settlement. They make trouble for us. They don't want us here."

Why?
Ahmed: "We are a nuisance to them. They want all our land for their own farming and they want complete control of all the archaeological sites here."

What can they do?
Ahmed: "They harass us ..."

Yes, we say, one of the children told us ...
Ahmed: "... they are always uprooting our olive trees, and in 2012 they began pumping raw sewage onto our fields. Those fields down there, right in front of us. It started to affect our olive and apricot trees."

Are there any other problems associated with the Israeli presence?
Ahmed: "Their presence has an effect on tourism too. It's a little complicated, but the town itself is in Area B. [Which the Oslo Accords placed under the joint control of the Palestinian Authority and Israel]. However, the major archaeological site on the hilltop is part of Area C, meaning it's under sole Israeli jurisdiction. The result of this to locals is that Israeli citizens can visit the site, but not the villagers, which means interaction with Palestinians is limited and tourist dollars hardly ever trickle down to local businesses.

"Another issue here is that Israeli tourists are only told ancient Jewish history and the

Part of the ancient site, with modern building behind

60

history of Christian and Muslim periods is completely neglected. In this way, Palestinian culture and contributions to the area's history are denied."

This site doesn't look particularly well-maintained. Is that a fair assessment?

Ahmed: "Yes. We can't touch it. We have no jurisdiction. And yes, the Israelis neglect it. Look about you ... Relics as old as time are everywhere and visitors can roam freely among the columns and remnants of walls, with no measures to safeguard these historical treasures from damage."

Is there a bright side to all this, Ahmed?

Ahmed: "In Sebastiya, the village's main mosque, known as the Nabi Yahya Mosque, stands inside the remains of a Crusader cathedral that is believed to be built upon the tombs of the prophets Elisha, Obediah, and John the Baptist ... right beside the public square. There are also Roman royal tombs, and a few medieval and many Ottoman-era buildings which survive in a good state of preservation. We have a lot to be grateful for ..."

The path leading up to the ancient site, with the hills beyond

GAZA

Background

The Gaza Strip, usually shortened to Gaza, is a tiny strip of land, (139 square miles or 360 square kilometers) wedged between Israel, Egypt, and the Mediterranean Sea. The population is around 1.6 million. Since 2006, Gaza has been governed by Hamas, whose military wing is listed as a terrorist organization by the United States, the European Union, and a number of other countries. In 2012, the United Nations recognized the Gaza Strip as part of the State of Palestine, claimed by the Palestinian Authority in Ramallah. However, owing to political disagreements on both the Israeli and Palestinian sides, and fighting between Palestinian factions inside Gaza, efforts towards Palestinian reconciliation, which would allow the merger of the Gaza and Ramallah administrations, have so far failed.

The border with Egypt is closed and Israel has command over the land border, the sea, and the air. Gaza is now virtually a prison.

Hamas rockets fired into southern Israel from Gaza have brought on attacks against Gaza. These attacks increased after Hamas's victory in the 2006 elections. Because Hamas's charter refuses to recognize the state of Israel, Israel refuses to recognize Hamas and has blockaded Gaza.

The worst conflict to date was the bombardment and invasion of Gaza carried out by Israel in the summer of 2014. This lasted approximately fifty days. The toll was over 2,200 Palestinians killed and 17,000 injured; 85 Israelis killed and 2,600 injured. The Palestinians killed were mostly civilians, including 513 children. The result is an already desperately poor Gazan population sliding towards disaster. Thirty percent of its population has been displaced, with large numbers taking shelter in UN-run schools. There are chronic shortages of services like electricity, water, and health provisions, and the housing shortage since 2014 has become acute. The damage to roads, buildings, hospitals, schools, water, and power supplies is so great that normal life is not possible.

TALKING TO CHILDREN IN GAZA—BEFORE THE JULY 2014 BOMBARDMENTS

Getting permission to enter Gaza on a research trip of this nature would have been very difficult, as Israeli permission is too unpredictable. Instead, Tamer in

Ramallah organized a video conference call with Tamer in Gaza. Following are conversations with children and some of the people who see and work with these children on a daily basis: trainers, teachers, and volunteers.

These adults work with the children on "life skills." These are skills you and I might take for granted, but for these children, locked into a brutal conflict not of their making, these are the skills they need to help them cope with what is going on around them.

These interviews took place a year before the July 2014 bombardment of Gaza. Interviews with Tamer workers and young people a year after the bombardment follow.

The children

There are about fifteen boys and girls in the room in Gaza, waiting to talk to us. They range in age from 10 to 14. Some of them are from Beit Hanoun in central Gaza. Nineteen people from this village were killed in the 2006 Israeli attack.

Wa'ad: "I am 10. I love living at Beit Hanoun. It's very close to the border with Israel, just 6 kilometers* away from the Israeli town of Sderot. It can be dangerous at times, being this close to the border, but I feel safe there. Does that make sense? It's good country. I've always lived there. It's my home."

Samia: "I don't feel safe there. Israel often attacks us. It's too close to them."

What is normal life for you?
Samia: "Football. There's a sports center in Beit."

Widad: "I am 9. I play football too. I can play anywhere, but I prefer to be goalkeeper."

What are some of the difficulties in your lives?
Samia: "The occupation. It fills our lives. We cannot escape it."

Shamad: "Israeli forces stole lots of land from Beit. Our family land was stolen …"

Shedah: "… Yes, the Israelis stole our family land too … in the east of Beit. It happened during the second Intifada. But at least we don't have contact with Israelis now. There's a safe zone, where nobody can go. It's only when they shell us that things are really difficult …"

*3.7 miles

Are any of your families separated from other family outside Gaza?

Etar: "My aunt left Gaza ten years ago and doesn't want to return. We can't visit her. We need permission ... It's very difficult. We are prisoners here really."

What do you think about your futures?

Samia: "I want to be a teacher, but I have other ideas too. Maybe to be a doctor. I want to help people. We need help here ... or an engineer to build Gaza another way."

How would being an engineer help?

Samia: "Engineers can help by giving people more houses, without money. It is very crowded here."

Nour: "I want to be a doctor, or a writer ... like you. I have written stuff about our homeland, and places like Syria and the Sudan. And I want to write about the last war of occupation, the first Intifada and how people are living in Gaza."

How are people living in Gaza?

Nour: "It's not living. We survive. Some families are separated and might never see each other again. It's too crowded here. There is no space and not enough housing for families. Everybody gets

tense, fights start. We are prisoners and have no control over our lives. We want the freedom to live our lives, that's all. Freedom to make our own choices ... our government here is not good too. They do nothing for us. Just talk. So, it's bad for us here ... and sometimes the Israelis attack. You see, we are in the middle?"

Samia: "... me too. I would tell people about how people are suffering here in the war, about kids killed by the Israelis. I would do this to show the world how people in Gaza have been affected by the war and the occupation. I would write about children's dreams, what it's like living in an occupied country and how kids suffer and dream of living without war ... in safety."

Shedah: "I'm happiest when I'm outside in a park. In nature. Living here is living in a prison. You can't go into the streets just like that. I want to find something that makes me happy."

Do you enjoy reading books?

Bar'a: "I like school lessons and reading stories. Everyone likes stories, don't they? I love them."

The children then had to go. Buses that

brought them here are waiting to take them home.

THE TAMER COORDINATORS

We talk to Ibrahim and Bataa, the co-ordinators present today.

Do any of the children have computers?
Ibrahim: "Most do, only a couple don't, but they get the use of one from a friend or relative. They like listening to music and playing games. They also use Skype to phone family and friends outside Gaza. They also have access to online studying. Sonia, for example, uses her uncle's Facebook account.

"They all love basketball. There's a court at the school, and some also play the piano or organ. They also play traditional games in the street when it's safe to go out. Games like hopscotch and marbles."

Can young people leave to study abroad?
Ibrahim: "Tradition prevents girls from traveling abroad. Boys can, in theory, get permission. But the permission almost never comes. It's up to the Israelis."

Have any of these children had family members arrested and taken away by the Israelis?
Ibrahim: "Yes, Ida's father was arrested and jailed for a year ... and Sondoz's uncle has been in prison for twenty years. He threw stones at Israeli troops during the First Intifada."

Bataa

Bataa Bleyan is a coordinator at The Family Center Project and Youth Program. He was keen to talk.

Can you tell us something about yourself?
"I work mainly with 15–18-year olds, but also deal with kids 6-18 overall."

Are we right in thinking that Tamer works to help children develop their personalities and in this way helps them become leaders in their communities?
"Yes. I think that is what we are trying to do. You see, children come up against different, even abnormal situations ... many negative things happen here. The abnormal becomes normalized. We try to move the child from being violent, angry, or depressed about this to something creative. We try and show them there is another way.

Many suffer from separation from family,

and from poverty. Being connected socially is crucial to us all, but these kids are often very disconnected, not physically, but socially and emotionally."

What are the causes of this disconnect?
"Broken marriages and aspects of our culture present difficulties. Marriages break up because of the stress of cramped accommodation and lack of privacy. There is also a lot of unemployment. In our culture, a man is not a man if he isn't working, supporting the family. Fathers are often angry. Children have to deal with these stresses as well as their own."

What about housing? Does this cause problems?
"It's a huge problem. Two or three generations often live in one small house, where all the possessions are shared. Recently, two members of a family were shot dead over a disputed cooking pot. 'We live like rats,' my father says.

"When violence is the norm the stress levels and tension are high. Those are the facts of life for most people in Gaza."

Do boys and girls have different problems?
"Yes and no. They have the same problems as everyone here, but they deal with them differently. The boys have more opportunity to express anger by fighting. Girls do not have this outlet ... and maybe this is cultural, so they tend to withdraw into themselves. They get depressed, inward looking.

"Boys also find it hard to focus. They tend to be overactive and violent. Girls suffer from feelings of isolation and aloneness. Most of them can't look a boy or man in the eye. They often find it very, very difficult to interact with others.

"After the attacks by Israel, in late December, 2012, we saw different behavior again. It's very clear the differences before and after an attack. After an attack, the kids don't talk of their dreams or hopes. They just can't or won't. They are nervous and angry. At times like this, they can't see a future and the longer it goes on the more ingrained these feeling will become. These kids do still have imaginations, but they have lost their childhoods ... they have been forced to think too much like adults."

What do you hope to achieve for the children?
"We are trying to get them back to their childhoods. They grow up too fast here. It's not natural or healthy."

What do you hope to achieve for yourself?
"To do something positive. Otherwise it can feel hopeless here sometimes."

Have you ever been outside Gaza?
"I went to Egypt once for a month, before the border was closed. Now it's not possible."

How do you see your future?
"I don't know really. Sometimes I think it will be all right one day, and at other times I feel it's all hopeless. I really don't want to be trapped here when I'm 60."

Bataa has to go, so we speak to Ahmed now, another Tamer volunteer.

Ahmed: "Three kids come to us from Beit Hanoun. A bus trip is a big deal for them. It's traveling ... it's magic for them. It gets them out of their prison feeling. Specially these kids, who live close to the Israeli lands, or near buffer zones.

"These children cannot have open, child-like minds. Their families live in constant fear and they pass this onto the kids. They don't let them do anything ... they're afraid something will happen to them. They watch them too closely.

"One boy came here, to town and saw a mannequin in a window and thought it was a woman. It is worse for the girls. It is both our customs and the situation together which make it difficult. They are prevented from participating in social life, stopped from going out.

"Recently, some German journalists came and they wanted to see anybody doing anything unusual ... anything new. They found a girl who played football. The only one in a team. Her name is Shaz and she's 22 or 23. I met her then. She said, 'I can do this regardless of whether people say it's abnormal ...' This is as wonderful as it is rare here: culture and war keep the children back."

What do you think is the main problem?
"Where to start. However, a huge problem is the fact that Gaza has been isolated for so long that cultural restrictions and leanings have been exaggerated. There is none of the cross-cultural mixing which healthy cultures experience.

"We can't even put boys and girls in the same study groups. If we try it, the families withdraw the girls. So, the girls lose out either way. But, we find that if we chip away at the children we can give them the tools to think differently. It takes time.

"We have these family centers so the families can see that what we are doing is not haram.*

"We have been encouraging them to write and it's starting to work better. They are writing short stories and poetry ... writing their memories. You can really sense from what they write how people in Gaza have been affected. We do our best to publish stuff for them. There are lots of accessible web-based media now. It cheers them to see their stuff 'out there' ...

"We also use YouTube. Sharida, a woman volunteer and I present stuff ..."

INTERVIEWS IN 2015
These discussions were conducted via video link between the UK and the Tamer Institute in Gaza in September, 2015.

Five young writers
For the security of those concerned there are no individual photos or last names.

These five young writers, aged between 20 and 24, were keen to talk to us. They were brought

*Forbidden under Islamic Law; sinful.

together by Ihab, the Tamer coordinator in Gaza. They are a loose group of committed people whose aims are the same. They want to keep Gaza in the eye of the world and to ensure that the young people they mentor and work with see the benefits of communicating their situation, via writing and digital platforms, to their own community and to a wider world.

The writers: two women, Ishraq, 24, and Rihan, 20; and three men, Mohanad, 22, Anas, 20, and Imad, 23.

Gaza has been described as a prison. Does it feel like that to you?
Ishraq: "Yes, we feel the loss of opportunities. There are armed soldiers all over the border and travel is near impossible. My sister was to take part in a conference in Tunisia, but the IDF (Israeli Defense Force) did not grant her a permit. We are being strangled. I am 24 and have never been out of Gaza. We lack experience and exposure to outside ideas and knowledge. A culture, I think, either progresses or dies. I think we are dying here."

Rihan: "It's not only outside invitations we can't accept, it's the fact that we cannot study abroad or take up scholarships. I think some of us are coming to believe we will spend our whole lives here in Gaza. Waiting, waiting … for permissions."

Ishraq: "Sometimes people get desperate and go out illegally … .and if they get caught and arrested, they just disappear. There are never any charges. The IDF call it 'administrative detention,' and they are released whenever it suits the IDF."

Anas: "This detention can be indefinite. Nobody can come in either, without permission. And I even know of some students who have got permission to go out, but their families are afraid they will not be allowed back in, so the families refuse them …"

Mohanad: "… And sometimes, students who have got permission to go out and study are not allowed back in. And who is to blame for this situation? Israel or our government? I have had many invitations and scholarship offers, but cannot take them up."

What, if anything, has changed since the assault last summer (July, 2014)?

Anas: "Nothing has changed for the better. Things are worse. Reconstruction is not possible, as materials are not allowed in. Schools, hospitals, and water and electricity supplies have also been badly affected. There are even fewer job opportunities now.

Over 200 schools were destroyed and some of those remaining have no roofs or are missing walls. In the winter it's wet and freezing and in the summer the heat is huge. The children also have psychological problems after the last bombardments, especially sleep problems, as the Israelis often bombed at night. Many of the damaged schools are being used as shelters for families whose houses were destroyed. These people are living miserable lives. There are also many people living in caravans. The heat is unbearable, but they cannot rebuild their houses. There are many street protests about these conditions."

Ishraq: "I have worked in East Gaza, the border area with Israel. This was the area worst affected in 2014. It was bad. Ambulances were not allowed in. It was considered just too dangerous even for them. Children witnessed children being killed and maimed. The IDF repeatedly told us it was safe there, but they targeted us. I was there. I saw this. Old people, women, and children, who had all come because they were told it was safe. Children saw this. Do you think they can forget these things? I work as a coordinator with families, to help alleviate stress. We do art and self-expression. It helps children, but it doesn't fix them. It doesn't make them children again."

What do you write? What do you want to say?

Ishraq: "I write for the many ... the many who are marginalized. So I can be their voice. I know this won't change much, but I write still; simply to give voice to what is happening. I insert what I write into different websites, like *Mondoweiss* [see the references at the back]."

Mohanad: "I have worked for Tamer for two years, as a coordinator for youth groups. And I write to act as a mirror on society, for the outside world. Many things are wrong, so I feel I have to write about what is in front of us here.

"During the latest attacks I wrote a Facebook page. I am not such a good writer, not eloquent you know, but I found the situation in 2014 so hard I felt it needed immediate action, an explanation. I have also written about people living in impossible situations in caravans, whole families. They boil in summer and freeze in winter. There is no rebuilding going on. There are no supplies.

"Some of us made an electronic book. This was with the help of iPal and supported by Tamer. The book is not published yet, but it sets out the 100 initiatives in Gaza since the assault of 2014 and contains articles, stories, and photos. It will be in English and translated into Arabic. It's for the world to see what is going on here. Our plan is to make it a monthly issue."

Rihan: "I am a student of English literature. I write for myself. I believe all Palestinians should write because people outside must wonder what exactly Gaza is. We need a 'show and tell' about Gaza, so the world can see what Gazans are suffering. I am going to write a section in the electronic book Mohanad mentioned. It will be specifically about how Gazan women's lives here have been affected."

Anas: "I am a second-year medical student. I am not a big writer. But when I start working as a doctor I can contact outside professionals and get help that way. We need physicians, nursing staff, and therapists especially. Maybe I can help in this way."

Imad: "I don't write, but am involved in two things at the moment. I have a job with Netketabi [see references]. This is a partnership with an NGO involved in sustainable development. The project aims to develop the Palestinian schools' curriculum, making interactive software suitable for smart devices like tablets, etc. Netketabi started five years ago in Palestine, but is now also here in Gaza. So far it has proved very popular with Gazans, but we need more support from the government and ministries. After the war, we had too many volunteers developing software and not enough support from the government. This project involves moving images; it's not just PDFs. We need the ministries to support us."

What difficulties do you face as writers?

Ishraq: "Not everyone in Gaza supports people who write, especially for political or financial reasons. Our two major difficulties here are that everyone now wants to write, and we do not have *reach out*, the channels to get our writing out into the world.

"There is not enough freedom of speech here in Gaza. I live in Gaza, so I am expected to support Hamas. I think Hamas feels that if the West Bank is to support Gaza then we must not criticize Hamas. Not everybody supports Hamas, but we have to be very careful. There just is not freedom of speech. This is the same in most Arab countries, I'm afraid. For example, Raif al Badawi, in Saudi Arabia [*www.amnesty.org.uk/Raif-Badawi*]. We feel real solidarity with him. He spoke out against his government. It's a risk here too. There are writers here who have been threatened and interrogated, even for Facebook entries.

"I had a friend here who wrote on Facebook that she was upset at how Hamas were treating her. Two days later we had to go to a place for interrogation. They asked us, 'Who do you work for?' and 'Who told you to say that?' That is one of the reasons Imad doesn't write, but he helps other children to write."

Why do you think it is important for children and young people to write?

Anas: "It's a way we can express ourselves. It's also a way the nation can express itself through its people, and children are people with a voice. Not enough proper attention is given to this area of our lives. Words help us express ourselves. Writing your thoughts and feelings, we think, is better self-expression than firing rockets. The rockets don't last; the words do."

Rihan: "I think children should be encouraged to write. They have unique voices with different points of view and stories to tell, especially to other children outside. Writing also helps them think about the reality of their lives. Helps them focus. These children have known nothing but war and the siege all their lives. It affects them."

Anas: "Drawing and writing both help children to relieve stress. Young adults need to share and writing gives them a way to do this. The Internet is such a blessing for us here. We must use it to our advantage, not just play around."

What are your ambitions for Gaza?
Mohanad: "I hope for a better leadership for our people. The situation here affects everything, even the beauty of the land and sea. I want Gaza to be free and hope we all get the opportunities we have been deprived of, for so long."

Rihan: "We need Gaza to be like a normal city, not a prison, with access to clean water, electricity, accommodation, sewage, and freedom of movement and speech."

Anas: "We want to live a free life like most of the world lives. The blockade should be ended. We want to live ordinary lives. Is that a lot to ask?"

Imad: "I hope I can help others to say whatever they want and reach out to the world. I'm working on it. Each of us has a small child inside us. Wish me good luck in freeing our children to live. Fear kills."

These writers/activists clearly articulate the difficulties and constraints under which Gazans live and the attendant difficulties of communicating the situation of their daily lives to the outside world, or even within their own community. Communication and contact are at the heart of their dilemma. They feel they operate in a void, and are determined to do whatever they can to overcome this.

The Tamer librarian—normalizing the abnormal
This discussion was conducted via video with the Tamer Institute in Gaza, in September, 2015.

Haneen is the librarian at the Tamer Institute in Gaza. She co-ordinates activities for children, aged 8-13, inside and outside the library. We spoke to her about the children she deals with day to day.

What are the most pressing social and behavioral issues you encounter?

"The older children tend not to focus on the chaos going on around them. They are happy to come here and draw, but their drawings display only darkness and a heaviness that we do not see when things are quiet in Gaza. They tend to draw in black and white; black planes, and dark clouds. They don't have very positive, fun ideas about life.

"However, the ones who are 6-8 years old tend to be more anxious if they are away from their parents. We are in a relatively safe part of Gaza here, so I was really surprised at how quickly, after the July 2014 bombardments, the children began appearing at the Centre again."

Do you see any gender differences in the way the children react to the situation?

"The boys pretend not to be afraid of the shelling, tanks, and planes. They have to be seen to be brave. The girls scream and hide under tables. Afterwards, when the shelling stops, the boys' games become more aggressive. They flare up more and fight. The girls retreat more. They go inside themselves. They have no real expression for how they feel. This is bad for them, I think."

What broad effects has the bombardment of 2014 had on the children's lives?

"In Gaza now, most children are just in the street playing. The education system is no longer serious. There is no money from local authorities to pay teachers, because the money is now going into rebuilding housing and infrastructure here in Gaza. But the biggest problem is that the Israelis freeze Palestinian assets. This delays payment of wages. The result is that teachers go unpaid and the children miss out. And since July 2014, many of the schools are crowded with refugees, so school is impossible for all these reasons. Even if they have a school to go to, there is no teaching.

"At the same time, UNWRA* has lowered its services and is not supporting teacher's salaries. This is because their money is going to help people fleeing Iraq and Syria at the moment."

How do the children think about the future?

"It's interesting. Children with older brothers and sisters tend to think about emigration or at least getting out for education at foreign universities. The younger ones, without older siblings, do

United Nations Works and Relief Agency

not think about the future. They think about the here and now."

Do the children engage with the outside world at all?

"We live in isolation. This is a prison, controlled by Israel on land, from the sea, and the sky. These children have no idea about the outside. Lots of the children who use their parents' computers only play games and talk to friends. They are locked out of the larger world. This is not healthy. They just want to play. I think it is their way of coping with a very uncertain life. And the games they play on the computer tend to be dark: war games, revenge games. The boys particularly want to strike back at Israel.

"These children have no peace inside themselves. They will sometimes talk of revenge, even the very young ones. One boy recently said to me, 'I will kill the Israeli people, as they are killing us now.'

"The only associations with Israel are hate-filled or fearful for these children."

Gazan children's drawings

Haneen: "These are drawings done by children aged 8-12. They were made in September, directly after the 2014 bombardments. I asked the children to draw something they were dreaming of right then. The picture with yellow color top and bottom is about kids crossing the road in front of an Israeli lorry.* The child said that he drew three blocks so the kids can walk safely away from the gun of the Israeli soldier. The rest of the pictures, especially the girls' ones, show simple dreams like getting a new house and enjoying the beauty of nature."

Child's drawing of crossing in front of Israeli lorry

*A lorry is a large truck.

GAZA

Gazan children's dreams of safety and play—not often their reality

Beit Ur School

Beit Ur al Tahta, Ur al Fauqa, and al Tireh are Palestinian villages in the Ramallah Governorate about 6.8 miles or 11 kilometers west of the city of Ramallah. Children from these three villages go to Beit Ur School, a co-educational secondary school for children from 11- to 17-years-old (fifth to twelfth grade).

Beit Ur al Tahta and Ur al Fauqa are close together, on one side of the Israeli Highway 443. Al Tireh is on the other side of this road and children from this village can only get to the school via a water drainage pipe that goes under the highway.

Bahan's story

"I get up early because I come to school on foot. I walk for 2 kilometers [1.24 miles]. I'm tired when I arrive. I come from the village over there, al Tireh …"

He points out of the window, beyond the security fence cutting off Highway 443, over the gorge to a small hilltop village.

"… I have to come through a pipe which was designed to carry water. It gets me under the highway. I do this every day. But I come. The pipe is better than before. It's safer now. The Israelis fixed it after we complained. It was too dangerous in the rainy season. The water used to rush through the pipe, completely filling it with fast water. They built a shelf of concrete, a ledge, which makes it safer, but it's still dangerous when there is heavy rain. The

Storm drain under highway used by children to get to school

76

pipe still gets full then. My father won't let me come if the rain is really heavy. I want to be here. At school, there are lessons and once a week, sports—football and volleyball—and my friends are here."

Anthony: I have struggled through the pipe myself. Access at both ends is outside the highway fence. The pipe runs under the road. The traffic above is deafening. I can easily see how rainwater could pour in a torrent down the hillside and into the pipe mouth, driven to higher and higher speeds down the hill and then funneling into a smaller pipe to become a surge. I would not like to be in there during heavy rain.

Access to the school for all the children and staff is difficult, indirect and in places dangerous.

Since the founding of the illegal Israeli settlement of Beit Horon in 1978 (current population 630), life for the school, the students, and staff of the Beit Ur School has been difficult.

The highway and the settlement dominate the Palestinian children's lives. They feel unwelcome, under threat in their own area.

Walking in through the main gate to the school and looking to the right, you see and hear Highway 443. There is a constant hum and roar of traffic. Access is barred by a high, wire fence. By car, the road itself can only be accessed via Israeli checkpoints.

On your left, a high concrete wall begins and curves around the settlement of Beit Horon. This wall encroaches on the school itself, surrounding the school on three sides. The highway makes up the only other view that is not the settler wall. It is a school hemmed in, a school under siege.

As you look across the highway and up to the hills, you can see ancient Arab land,

The settler highway seen from the front gate of the school

Part of the settler wall and fence seen from the school

and the village of al Tireh, but the highway acts as a breaker from this view. It also acts as a reminder that this is occupied country and that this school's position and future are very delicately balanced ... and one wrong move could tip the balance against them.

We have come to speak to the students who have said they would like to talk to us. They speak to us mostly in good English, with some help from Juwana, our guide and interpreter from the Tamer Institute. There are thirteen girls: Rand, Simah, Raneen, Mayar, Jinan, Meera, Haneen, Nadeen, Najd, Nawras, Amal, Da'd, and Ru'a—and three boys: Jad, Baha, and Adam. All are aged 14-15.

Can you think of one word that best describes how you feel about school?
They come up with these words: beautiful, important, hope, dreams, amazing, future. They also agree, laughing, that it's sometimes boring.

Tell us about school life.
Many shout out: "It's hard."

How?
Mayar: "The road is too long to walk. And we are surrounded by a huge, concrete wall, so we have to go the long way round. In winter it's freezing and in summer there is no shade."

Haneen: "We get afraid. The occupation is everywhere. The settlers make us afraid. They come to our school with their weapons. It's scary ..."

Rand: "They come when they like. They don't give reasons. Maybe to make us hate coming to school. But we are all determined to come to school."

Jinan: "We have been stopped on our way sometimes. Settlers jump out at us and shout in Hebrew. We don't understand, but their faces are full of hate. They just harass us."

The settler road, only access to school and home

Meera: "Sometimes, we are afraid they will kill us ..."

Jad: "Sometimes they make noise so we can't hear in class. They sound very loud alarms. They do this once or so every three weeks. We never know when ..."

Juwana, our guide and interpreter, explained that when the settlers have holidays or feast days they use very loud horns or sirens; and there is also the constant noise from the traffic.

How do you get to school?

Everybody shouts at once. What was generally agreed was that, apart from the pipe under the highway, the distances they had to travel to school were too great, given there was no public transportation, and

Anthony and Annemarie: We have walked on this road and it is dangerous. There are many blind curves and the road is narrow, wide enough only for one car.

Anthony: I stood in the middle of this road, with what I thought was enough visibility to be safe. I wasn't. A jeep suddenly appeared from nowhere, at great speed, and I had to pin myself up against the rock face. It is also an incredibly steep road in places.

For the aged, or mothers with young, it must be like playing Russian roulette. The Israelis built the road to serve the settlement and, in so doing, cut the villagers off from traditional trackways and roads.

the road itself was too narrow and winding to take a rest in safety. They also reported that the blind curves make oncoming cars invisible, and near-collisions are common. And to top it all off, they also fear the settlers, especially those who are armed, who sometimes abuse them on the road.

Can you describe a normal day?

Baha: "We start the day with three or four lessons and then have a break for breakfast. Then we have a few more lessons, then back home, through the pipe. I go hiking in the hills a lot and visit my friends in the village. I get on Facebook too

The class we interviewed

and watch TV. There is an afternoon club in the village, but I don't go. I'm usually too busy with school work and friends."

Meera: "I get up and I eat breakfast. I come to school by car. We live on this side of the highway. At the start of the day, we line up and listen to the Palestinian national anthem and have a reading from the Koran. I have the same lessons as Baha. When I get home I study, watch TV and listen to music …"

Who has a computer at home?
Everybody.

What do you do on your computers?
Haneen: "I have Facebook friends in other Arab countries, and in Cyprus and a girl from Argentina. She requested me so she could learn about Palestine."

Jad: "I have a friend from Egypt …"

Simah: "Me from Sri Lanka, India, Syria, Egypt, and Korea … and Lebanon and China."

Why do you have so many contacts in other countries?
The general consensus is that they want to see if these places are like they appear on TV, and to improve their language and exchange information about ways of living.

Mayar: "When we tell Facebook friends about our situation, they say it sounds like war. They see we are not living in peace …"

How do you feel about the Wall and the security fence?
Jad: "I feel controlled … in my own country."

Haneen: "Like toys in a box."

Raneen: "That it is not fair …"

Meera: "Depressed and upset. I like open places. There's no peace here."

Baha: "I don't feel anything anymore … It's just there, but it's too noisy. Sometimes we can't hear the teacher. It's hopeless. Better to feel nothing."

Jad: "It makes me feel fear."

What's your best day?

Jad: "When we visited the sea. I didn't sleep the night before I was so excited ... and when they release prisoners ... and when I meet old friends."

Rand: "When I can visit the family land, but it's difficult because of security problems. I have been once only."

Adam: "When I go through the checkpoint and into Jerusalem to visit the Dome of the Rock. I did it once."

Meera: "Every summer when we go to visit refugee relatives in Jordan."

Baha: "I went to a summer camp in Cyprus once. It was brilliant."

What are your hopes and plans for the future?

There is the usual list of professions such as doctor, engineer, scientist, journalist, lawyer, and so on. But what is paramount for them is the freedom to move about in their own country, with no more occupation, and peace for everybody.

Have any members of your families suffered during the occupation?

Amal: "My father was in prison for a year, when he was very young. He was arrested during the 2002 invasion. They took lots of people. My brother was also taken for throwing stones at the soldiers."

Baha: "Two of my cousins have been in prison ... during 2002."

Haneen: "An uncle of mine was murdered in Jordan, before I was born, by the Israelis. Nobody knows why."

Raneen: "My aunt was injured by a settler's car on that road we were talking about."

Rand: "My uncle was killed, when he was 6, in a car accident with settlers. He was coming to school when it happened."

Baha: "Don't ask us any more questions about family problems. It's too depressing."

Is there anything else you would like to say?

They told us then that they had written stories in English, which they wanted to show us—you can see Rand's story and extracts from some of the others on the next page. Rand read hers out. She also showed us a board she had made, a collage of wild flowers ... the theme of her story.

RAND

Don't pick wild flowers

Spring came soonly after the cold winter, which makes us suffer on our way to school or return back home.

In Spring we feel happy, spending time smelling different kinds of flowers. On our way home from school, each one of us had their own flower that others must not pick or smell. So each flower took the name of one of us. All of us respected the rule. Every day we leave our flowers moving gently, as we wave our hands goodbye.

We saw a street sign, 'Don't pick wild flowers'. Who wrote that? Who put it there? None of us knew.

One day when we started smelling our flowers on our way back home, we saw Israeli soldiers holding weapons. Others driving bulldozers digging the ground there. They didn't notice or care about our flowers that died there under the wheels of the bulldozer and boots of the soldiers. They removed the sign and threw it away.

I reached home with sadness.

In the next days the same thing was repeated, but the soldiers also started building a huge, concrete wall around the site of our wild flowers.

Spring ended and so did the school year.

In the next school year we were very sad that the road to school was changed and a new one made, surrounded by a huge concrete wall. We now had a school captured by a wall on three sides. We still imagine our wild flowers, which we are sure the Israeli wall killed. But the wall is unable to kill the smell of our lovely wild flowers.

NAJD

I start my day with hope to make all hard things easier, but ask, "why did they build a wall round us?"...I have hope. Palestine is in my blood and soul. Nothing will change that forever...

AMAL

Tears, blood, wounds and pain summarise the life of the Palestinian people who are still suffering from the practices of the Israelis. People who have tasted the bitterness of lost loved ones will remain steadfast in face of occupation.

NADEEN

The children of Palestine wake up to the sound of bullets and the noise of soldiers. The world's children go to school in morning full of life and hope and optimism. This is the meaning of childhood. But the children of Palestine go to school psychologically smashed, full of anxiety and pessimism. It fills our souls. It is the occupation that fills the streets and us. It is the apartheid wall round our school that cuts us in half,...the settlers behind the wall and adjacent to our school and their barbaric behavior. They harass us daily both in the morning and in the afternoon...swearing and shouting.

JAD

At summer we decided to go on a journey to Haifa, Acre and Jaffa, cities occupied by Israel. But first we had to make a permit to be allowed to get inside occupied Palestine. I was excited and I really wanted to see and swim in the Mediterranean. After two weeks we had our permit, but my dad didn't get his permit. I don't know why. They never tell us these things. I felt sad because my dad won't be able to go with us in this journey.

SEMA

... but in my country I saw the Israeli flags everywhere. I saw in my country others enjoy the fruits we deprived. I looked in my country and see alien strangers. In my country I saw remnants of the old houses inhabited by our ancestors placed upon them Hebrew words and phrases and Israeli flags. My country, which I must get permit to visit.

HANEEN

At the check points they say you can enter or not. The soldiers scream at old people and children in their faces and threaten them with dogs.

All this and more is our daily life, but our determination to stay in this land drives them crazy, so we visit new places in our territory from time to time to remember and learn about the places we still do not know in our own land.

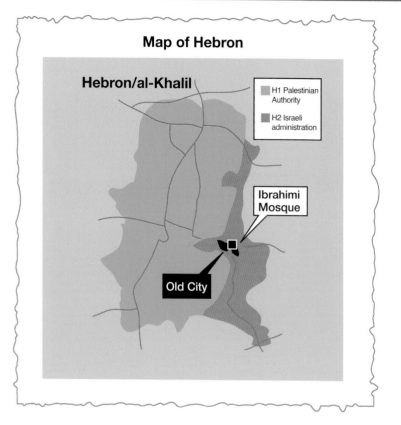

Map of Hebron

Hebron/al-Khalil

H1 Palestinian Authority

H2 Israeli administration

Ibrahimi Mosque

Old City

THE CITY OF HEBRON

Hebron is located in the southern West Bank, 18.6 miles or 30 kilometers south of Jerusalem. It is the largest city in the West Bank, and the second largest in the Palestinian Territories, after Gaza. It is a busy center of West Bank trade, with a population of approximately 250,000.

It is a holy city for both Jews and Muslims because of its association with Abraham, and the Al-Ibrahimi Mosque in the Old City is an important site for both religions.

Hebron is different from other Palestinian cities in that it has Israeli settlers living in the heart of its built-up area, right next to, and indeed on top of, Palestinians. There are around 600-800 settlers in four settlements within the city, close to Shuhada Street in the old quarter. Some of the houses are built on top of the old market, and wire netting protects

Wire mesh in Old City market protecting those below from missiles and rubbish thrown by settlers

One of the checkpoints for entry to Old City

the Palestinians in the market alleys from the rubbish, and other things, thrown down by the settlers. The site of these settlements is a daily reminder to Palestinians that they are occupied, as is the presence of around 1,500 Israeli Defense Force soldiers, who are there to look after the interests of the settlers.

After the Six-Day war of 1967, Israel took control of the whole city. In 1997 they withdrew from much of the city,

but it is now divided into two sectors: H1, controlled by the Palestinian Authority and H2, roughly 20% of the city, administered by Israel. The settlers are governed by their own authority, the Committee of the Jewish Community of Hebron. This arrangement means the settlers are outside Palestinian law.

PROBLEMS

The problems caused by this situation have been documented by a number of organizations and individuals, many of them moderate Jews living abroad, or Israelis themselves.

The Israeli human rights organization B'tselem (www.btselem.org) says that "grave violations of Palestinian human rights have occurred in Hebron" because of the "presence of the settlers within the city." B'tselem cites regular incidents of "almost daily physical violence and property damage by settlers in the city."

In 2001 a Human Rights Watch report concluded that Israeli authorities consistently failed to investigate or prosecute crimes committed by settlers against Palestinians.

We had heard that tensions were high between the settlers and the Arab population in Hebron. We came to see for ourselves—to talk to children and see in what ways they might be affected by this situation.

We found a bustling West Bank city: shops, street food hawkers, traffic, noise, and the rattle of a working city. What we quickly

Rabbi John Rosove, Senior Rabbi, Temple of Israel, Hollywood, visited Hebron with a group of US Jews in 2013. He talks, in his blog, of what they found:

Our group visited H2 with David Wilder, the spokesman for the Hebron Jewish community.

Wilder is a religious settler who packs a pistol on his hip over which is draped his tzitzit.* He is a passionate defender of the religious right of Jews to Hebron. He says there is no such thing as the Palestinian people, that the Arabs there have no distinct identity separate from Arabs in the Middle East, and that they have contributed nothing of lasting value to the advancement of civilization, in contrast to Judaism and the Jewish people.

While denying Palestinians their national identity he demands that they recognize our Jewish religious and national rights …

Wilder denies that he is an 'extremist'! Palestinians and most Israelis don't agree.

He opposes a two-state solution, and when challenged by evidence of settler and Israeli mistreatment of Palestinians, he said these are lies disseminated by anti-Israel and anti-Semitic groups.

*Tzitzit refers to a fringe, tassel, or decorative cord worn by Jewish males on traditional garments.

felt was the discomfort and tension in parts of this city.

We found access to the mosque intimidating; stony-faced soldiers with automatic weapons. The afternoon we went through the checkpoint, two Arab girls were harassed, delayed, and generally humiliated on their way to the mosque, by the Israeli Defense Force personnel who act as security guards.

We were to see similar incidents going through the checkpoint to visit the Cordoba School where we would interview children. We would be told of countless other incidents by the children we would meet, and by their teachers.

Children living under occupation.

This is the background to Hebron today. This is the city where we were to meet school children and ask them what it is like to live here.

What we found at the school
We were half-expecting a grim place, full of enmity and anger, or at least anger about the settlement, which the school overlooks.

Checkpoint for entry to Shuhada Street leading to Cordoba School

This is what we found at the school, some of it very surprising and the more wonderful for that.

THE CORDOBA SCHOOL: A SCHOOL UNDER SIEGE

The school caters to girls from grades one to ten (5 to 15 years of age) and boys up to the age of 12. There are currently 175 pupils; 92 are girls.

The street that leads to the school is barricaded off from the town by huge, concrete blocks and very clear "no go" signs. We walk up this ordinary enough looking street with its housing on the left and a high, rock wall on the right. The Cordoba School sits atop this wall.

We are told the houses are almost all deserted. The former Palestinian occupants have fled after trouble with the settlers, who live only a street away. At the end of the street we go through an Israeli checkpoint. This is the route the children take to and from school every day. It is scary. The school itself, above street level, overlooks settler buildings, including a synagogue.

This is a school on the edge.

We are greeted by Nour Nasar, the headmistress. She explains that the children must start class early, 7:30, and finish by 12:30. This is to avoid settler children, who bully them on the way to their own school at 8:00 and when they leave at 1:00.

Would you like to tell me about your job?
Nour Nasar: "Last week was Passover for the Jews, so the rules changed every day. The Israeli Security called every day with instructions about times. One day they called and simply said, 'Today you finish at 10:30' and hung up."

She shrugs, smiles and hands us over to two teachers who take us to meet some children.

There are eighteen children in a semi-circle in the room. The girls are aged from 13 to 15, and the boys are 11 and 12.

The boys are Hamdi, Salah, Abdallah, Mowaliya, Malik, Hussain, and Shahrukh. The girls are Bilan, Shehad, Jaimah, Yara, Saya, Shada, Reyhab, Anor, Samah, Ayah, and Marian.

Some of the children speak English, others speak through an interpreter.

What are the troubling things in your lives?
Samah: "I feel afraid sometimes. Threatened and scared. It's an everyday worry. Whether anything happens or not … it's there. I don't know what to expect when I come out of the house. When I cross the barrier at the end of the street I sometimes meet settlers and they stone and curse us. Sometimes it's settler children who do it, sometimes adults."

Ayah, a 15-year-old girl: "Sometimes settlers bring dogs to hassle us on our way."

Malik, an 11-year-old boy: "I've also been hassled by dogs. I asked them why they were doing this and they just replied, 'The dogs are friendly.'"

Ayah: "Sometimes we have to leave early if the settlers are celebrating a feast day or something. They say they don't want to see us."

Mowalya, a 12-year-old boy: "Last year my older brother, Ahmed, was leaving school with some friends and some settler children started pushing them. The security arrived and said it was the Palestinian children who started the trouble.

"So they took them away, separated them and questioned them. The kept them for a whole day. At the end of the day my grandfather went and collected them. Before they left, the soldiers hit them with rifle butts and told them never to attack settler children again. They had to sign a paper saying if they got caught again, they would have to pay a fine of 2,400* shekels. They took their photos and fingerprinted them all. We can't even defend ourselves."

What's a good or bad day for you?
Shahrukh, an 11-year-old boy: "I love Fridays when the whole family goes out of town. We go to our village."

Bilan, 14-year-old girl: "We have some land with fruit trees and vegetables. All the eight children go. We have a picnic. We take

*In US dollars, approximately $618.

walks. I can breathe there. The air is fresh and there are no soldiers. I hate Fridays at home. The Israelis and Palestinians clash usually. There are always gas attacks, hassles ... nothing is simple."

Samah: "The Jews have a lot of celebrations. Just in front of the barrier usually. They come out on the streets playing very loud music. This often happens at exam time. It's impossible to concentrate. They have music and dancing ... and they drink and lose control and behave badly. When they're drunk they run around knocking on doors, making trouble."

Yara, a 16-year-old girl: "My favorite day is Thursday. I love it. I come out of school and visit my grandfather on the other side of Hebron, away from the settlers."

Reyhab, a 11-year-old boy: "I live out of town a little. We have land. I wake up every day at 7:00. That's when the diggers start. They come and dig up everything we plant. We used to have cherry and almond trees. The land is now flat, empty. They say it's a heritage area. They are digging for archaeology. They put a caravan on our land. They say engineers are looking for artifacts. Our house is near their

The settler synagogue as seen from Cordoba School

to cross the barrier to go to the shops. It's a quick trip normally. Then, suddenly, they close the barrier. They don't give reasons or tell us how long it will be closed. If I am out for a long time, my family worry. One day I was with a friend, she is bigger, and she tried to push through the barrier. A soldier pushed her and threw tear gas between us. She couldn't breathe and she got burned from the tear gas. They kept her there for more than an hour, then told her to take another route home. The barrier can stay up for 4-5 hours. It's up to them."

synagogue. They drink and throw bottles at our windows."

Hussain, a 12-year-old boy: "I live on the other side of Hebron. My mother is a teacher at this school. One day I was leaving school on my own and I met a settler on the stairs onto the street. He punched me in the stomach and ran away. I was afraid. As he was running away, the settler called out, 'You homo,' to me. He said it in English. In our culture this is a very bad thing to say. The worst insult. Another settler threw spirits* over a friend of mine too."

Ayah, a 15-year-old girl: "Sometimes I have

Alcohol like vodka and whisky.

Jaimah, a 15-year-old girl: "I used to be at another school, behind the barrier. I had to wait every day at a friend's house for my father to collect me. Security said I could not go alone. One day I did, I went by myself, and they threw tear gas at me and I got burned."

Ayah: "One day I was out with some friends and some Palestinian boys started throwing stones at the soldiers. The soldiers started firing bullets. We were in the middle of this. We had to stand up against a wall to keep away from the bullets."

What are your hopes for your future?
Anor, a 14-year-old girl: "I'd like to be a journalist one day. But most, I want to

live away from Hebron. I don't want my children to suffer as we do."

Samah: "I'd love to have freedom of movement in the future ... no barriers. To come to school knowing my day is full and settled, not affected by restrictions and violence. One of my hopes is to travel all over Palestine without permits. I dream of visiting Gaza and all of Palestine."

Bilan: "One day, I was walking with my cousin and some settler boys sprayed something on us. I was lucky, but my cousin's hair was burned and it all fell out. What if it had hit our eyes? I want to be an astronomer and get out of Hebron."

Malik: "I want to be an engineer. And I want to stay here and live in a liberated Palestine. I'm sick of living with violence and hearing about prisons. I want to travel around Palestine, visit Jerusalem. I want to be without fear. You know, every now and then soldiers come, after midnight, to search houses. They turn everything upside down ..."

Why do they search your houses?
Abdallah: "They say someone in the area threw stones at them. So they search everybody. They smell all the children's hands to see if they've held stones."

Bilan: "Once the soldiers searched our house and pushed everybody into one room. They locked us in. They used the rest of the house for themselves and left in the morning. Once, my father tried to stop them from entering. They hit him on the chin with a rifle butt."

Shada, a 16-year-old girl: "One day last summer, the army kicked on all the doors in our neighborhood. Then they shouted through a loudspeaker for us all to leave our houses. They ordered us to stand by the barrier with our hands up, even pregnant women and children. This went on from 7:00 until 9:00 PM ..."

How do the children cope with all this?
Shada, one of the support staff present: "We set up a library outside the school area. We worked hard to get the children to come and to work and forget the fear for a bit. To get it out of their systems, for a while anyway. It was hard at first; their parents were afraid. But now there's good participation."

We thank the headmistress and leave. The children have been very honest and open with us. They might not be happy about their situation, but they do not seem cowed.

We found anger and a wish for the settlers and their IDF protectors to go away, but we also found great charm, clarity, and acceptance without surrender. Their situation, they felt, was the way things were. Things were mostly outside of their control, but this was not the way it had to remain. It seemed to us they had a burning love of their country and simply wanted it back: a common enough theme all over Palestine. But they also wanted a future not made ugly by the tensions and inequalities of occupation. Like all of us, they had dreams.

Entrance to the Hebron Youth Development Resource Centre

THE HEBRON YOUTH DEVELOPMENT RESOURCE CENTRE

The Hebron Youth Development Resource Center (YDRC) is a community center for Palestinian youth. Here young people meet friends, find books, get adult support, and take part in various cultural activities in a safe environment.

The day we arrived they were preparing for such an event.

Walking in here is a vastly different experience to entering Cordoba School. This is not a school blighted by proximity to settlers or separated off. This part of Hebron at least, feels like what it is, a busy, active city.

The teenagers we meet seem more relaxed, confident.

We talk to nine girls, aged 14-15, about their lives in Hebron. They are all from the same school, and are due to sit the International Baccalaureate,* or, as it is commonly known, the "IB," in three-years' time.

They are: Abeer, Asma, Qamar, Dawlah,

*The "IB" offers internationally recognized educational programs for students aged 3-19. There are nearly 4,500 schools worldwide offering these programs.

Alya, Leen, Mays, Orouba, and Newan.

A question for you all … why do you come to the Center?
"To be with friends," a lot of them shout.

Can you tell me what a normal day for you is like?
Leen: "Not much really. I get up, go to school, come home, study … sometimes I play football. That's it. I like the weekend best. I travel into Palestine with my family then. Sometimes we go to Jericho or to land we own outside Hebron. We do BBQs and read, take photos, play. It's peaceful."

Mays: "I watch a lot of Indian movies. There's a Bollywood channel. I also read a lot of novels, Arabic and English. I like going on school trips. March and April are best. We go to Jericho and Tulkarem and to fun fairs."

Newan: "I like the weekend best. I chat a lot on Facebook."

Can you describe a difficult day?
Qamar: "When I get my grades and they are bad. My parents deprive me of lots of things, like they block Facebook and I'm not allowed to visit friends, have to do more chores at home and sometimes they take my mobile. Another bad day is when my mother interferes with what I wear."

Abeer: "When I was 12, my sister got a job in a hospital in Jenin. She took me with her, I didn't need an ID, but they turned me back at the checkpoint. They didn't give a reason. I was really disappointed. That was a bad day."

Do you go to Al Ibrahim Mosque?
Alya: "No. My mother says it is dangerous. There are too many Israeli soldiers and a checkpoint into the Old City. Settlers, they are the worst, the most aggressive to us."

Does anybody else have problems going to the Mosque?
Abeer: "The soldiers stop us and search us. They keep us behind the checkpoint for a

Checkpoint for Palestinians to enter Al Ibrahimi mosque

long time ... in the sun. When we get inside the mosque we can only see a small part because of the division."

Leen: "I have an aunt who lives in the Old City. Sometimes the soldiers say she is not allowed into the mosque after midday. The Jewish people come in then."

Newan: "The Israelis say that all Muslims can visit Al-Aqsa Mosque at Ramadan, but really, they only let women and children. They didn't allow me the first time I applied, but then they did. I loved it. It is a wonderful experience."

Are you comfortable walking around the streets?

All the girls agree that they get some trouble from Palestinian boys. Asma says, "The boys say things we don't like."

Have any of your family had problems?

Asma: "I don't want to talk about that. We've had too many."

Alya: "One of my relatives, a distant cousin, was charged with throwing stones. This was in 2000, during the Second Intifada. He was 18 at the time and they sentenced him to five years in prison. It was a waste of his life."

Qamar: "Our neighbor, Shirbit, was not a young man. He has a family, two children. He went to university to study chemistry. He was charged with the intention to make bombs—just because of the subject he was studying. He got a twenty-five-year sentence ... just for studying."

The only boy in the group!

What hopes do you have for the future?

Leen: "I would like to study abroad and follow my father's footsteps. He's a medical equipment engineer. But I wouldn't leave until Palestine is liberated. The Israelis might not let me back."

Orouba: "I want to be a journalist."

Abeer: "I want to become a fashion designer and would love to study design abroad ... and then start a fashion design business here or in Bethlehem. I follow a lot of trends and get ideas on the Internet."

Mays: "I dream to go to Japan to study. But my mother said I would go mad. How does she know? Anyway, I switched to chemistry, but my father says I would just be arrested!"

All suddenly laugh and tell us they all want to meet Justin Bieber.

Newar: "I want to go to Chad in Africa. It's rich in nature."

Abeer: "I would like to spend a month discovering new places and countries."

Newar: "I would love to see all Palestine ... to see what others are allowed to see. But we can't travel where we want. We need permits and they are difficult."

Would anyone like to say anything else?
They all wanted us to tell them about the book we planned. We explain our intentions to let Palestinian children tell their stories.

Newar: "Can I tell you about our council?"

Yes, of course.
Newar: "We, young people, have a council here in Hebron. We can be heard. Those in power listen to us."

Diala (a librarian at the Center): "Not all children in Hebron are heard."

Abeer: "I can only judge for myself, not for all children, but I think we have lots of places and opportunities. Probably, all children in Hebron do not have these opportunities. Do you know, two girls were killed last week. They were 14 and 20. They were shot in their field. The case is closed. Nobody cares about finding the truth."

The librarian and the girls we interviewed at the Centre

These are the thoughts of young people who seem to be under less pressure. They also do not live in daily contact with Jewish settlers. But they still live in an occupied city and country. The last comment, about the two girls who were shot dead last week, shows how even these young people are affected by the occupation and the sometimes random, unchecked violence.

HEBRON

We take group photos, thank everybody, and leave. Outside is buzzing. The event is shaping up and rehearsals are in full swing outside the Centre: music, a play, and general celebration of the arts. We head back to Ramallah.

Entrance to Community Center study and resource areas

Burj al Luq Luq was set up in 1991 as a community center for the Palestinian inhabitants of the Old City of Jerusalem. The Center runs programs for women, children, and adolescents. It is situated in the Bab Hutta neighborhood, on a hilltop inside the Muslim Quarter of the Old City, where the northern and eastern walls of the Old City meet. The Center overlooks the Dome of the Rock, a symbol to Muslims, Jews, and Christians alike.

Burj al Luq Luq has the largest play and sports facilities for young people in East Jerusalem. In 2007, the Israeli authorities served demolition orders on six of the Center's buildings. A popular protest by both Palestinians and Israelis put a stop to this. However, those running the Center know that their position is uncertain. They know the battle over their land has only been postponed.

We meet Fida at the Damascus Gate, outside the Old City, and walk off together to the Center.

When we get there we are greeted by one of the volunteers, Al Mushina.

What are the Center's aims?
Al Mushina: "We want to create safe and healthy playgrounds for the children of the Old City ... and provide a breathing space for adults from the small and crowded housing units they live in.

We also want to develop educational, cultural, psychological, health, and entertainment programs for the teenagers and adults of the Old City, and, most importantly at the moment, we need to protect the land from any Israeli settlement plans in the future.

And, the families that come to the Center are originally from here. The kids use it as an after school club. They don't have access to any other such facilities in their area. This is an important place for them."

What do they do while they are here?
Al Mushina: "They read stories and play sport ... they all love basketball. They watch videos about nature, about Palestine, and about other children. And teachers also give their time to talk to the children ... doing remedial work on math, Arabic, and some English. We do a lot of extra support work round literacy and writing skills too. Most of the children come to about three sessions per week, but we are open all week. It's open access."

Taseem (another volunteer): "... and I do handicrafts with them..."

Where is the funding from?
Taseem: "France ..."

There are eight children here today, all girls. Ramin, who is 7; Meisa and Ragda, who are 9; and Besan, Nibras, Ablaia, Nadim, and Mira, who are 10. They have asked not to have their photos taken.

Can you tell us something about yourselves?
Meisa: "I am 9. I like swimming best, but there is no pool here. I have been

swimming at Jericho, but I can't swim in Jerusalem. The pools are too expensive."

Nibras: "I like drawing best. Drawing houses, people and the Al Aqsa Mosque here in the Old City."

Ragda: "I like painting best."

Do you have computers at home?
They all do.

What do you use them for?
Taseem, the volunteer: "They play games on them and do searches for homework and stuff. And they go on Facebook ..."

Who has Facebook friends?
A lot of shouting and arm waving. It turns out they have between 50 and 250 Facebook friends each.

Who has a mobile phone?
Only Nibras and Ramin do.

Ramin: "I saved from pocket money to buy mine. I use it to contact parents and friends. We use SMS a lot ... it's cheaper."

What do you like about living in Jerusalem?
Besan: "I can go to the Al-Aqsa Mosque."

Meisa: "I like the Center here."

Ablaia: "I like the Church of the Holy Sepulchre best."

Is there anything you don't like about Jerusalem?
Nibraj: "Israeli soldiers. They came to our house and took away my 18-year-old brother. They say he threw stones at them. He has been in prison for a year. We are from Silwan."

Abla: "We have nowhere to go, except home, and our houses are so small and crowded. And we can't travel. It's very difficult for us to travel. They make it almost impossible."

Where would you like to travel to, that you can't?
Abla: "Jordan, Gaza, and Lebanon. We are not allowed by the authorities."

Tell me about your houses?
Besan: "We have two rooms. We have a bathroom inside, so we have one room for everything else. And I have one sister and two brothers and my parents."

Ablaia: "We have three rooms and we are three daughters and my parents."

Meisa: "We have three rooms. And there are seven children and my parents."

Silwan is outside the southeast walls of the Old City of Jerusalem. It has been a farming village since the medieval period, as it has easy access to a natural spring. The village was designated an exclusively Palestinian neighborhood after the Arab-Israeli war of 1948. In the 1990s, Israeli settler families began to move into the area. This has been declared illegal by the United Nations.

After the 1948 war, the village came under Jordanian occupation, and this rule lasted until the Six-Day war of 1967. Since that time, it has been occupied by Israel. Silwan is administered as part of the Jerusalem Municipality. In 1980 Israel, without formally annexing it, incorporated East Jerusalem (of which Silwan is a part) into its claimed capital city of Jerusalem. The international community has declared this to be illegal.

Depending on how the neighborhood is defined, the Palestinian residents in Silwan number 20,000 to 50,000, while there are about 500 Israelis.

Many Palestinians from Silwan have been arrested. The area is coming under increasing pressure from Israeli settlers, who seem intent on taking over the whole of the city of Jerusalem.

Does anybody else have reasons for not liking it in Jerusalem?

Mira: "I can go swimming in the YMCA, but many of my friends can't. It's too expensive for them."

Nadim: "When guys get arrested ..."

Mira: "... my brother got arrested, but came out after a week and he was expelled from Jerusalem for fifteen days. They said he had thrown stones, but when they looked at the photos they saw that it wasn't him, so why did they banish him from Jerusalem for fifteen days?"

Nadim: "... Yes, my brother-in-law was arrested too, for throwing stones. They kept him in for a couple of days, then let him go. They said it wasn't him. Well, he knew that."

What makes your parents unhappy about living here?

Shahed, an 11-year-old boy, has just come in: "My parents get really upset when the Israelis start arresting people and when homes are built or renovated in our area by settlers, without permission. We have to get permission for any changes to our homes, but Israelis can do what they like. It was the same near Ramallah too, my

Community Centre Youth Day celebrations

parents said. And when soldiers enter Al-Aqsa Mosque and arrest people, throw stones, or when other 'accidents' happen there."

Taseem: "In 2011, the Israelis wanted to take over parts of Silwan. They got a court order saying it was okay, but there was a huge protest, by many Israelis too, and it has been 'postponed.'"

What do you want to do when you finish school?

Another new arrival, Shlad, a 10 year-old boy, speaks up ...

Shlad: "I want to study social sciences or psychology."

Besan: "I want to be a painter. I want to paint our people."

Ablaia: "I want to be a dentist."

Mira: "I want to run my own beauty center."

Ranim: "I want to be a teacher."

Seema: "... a children's doctor."

Nadim: ".... a doctor or dentist."

Tuis (a newcomer, a girl of 11): "I want to be a painter."

Maisa: "... an architect."

If you could change three things, what would they be?

Shehad: "No more police ... more success in my studies and let me see my dreams."

Mira: "I want to see my dreams too.... that nobody takes Al-Aqsa from us ...and I want to see my five brothers to have fewer problems and to succeed."

Tuis: "For the police to leave my brothers alone. All five have been arrested at different times. ...to see us all have the chances to succeed."

Ablaia: "I don't want the Dome of the Rock to be ruined ... and I would like to see a temple put in place there ... a mosque."

Nibras: "I want freedom for my brothers ... and the freedom to stay and live in Silwan. It is my home, but the Israelis want it for themselves."

We ask the girls if this is a good place for them to come. The roundtable consensus is that it is good at the Center because here they can play outside. Where they live, their parents will not allow them to play in the street. They are afraid for them. The Center is a haven for them.

A lot of you have mentioned problems your brothers have with the Israeli authorities. Why is this?

Mira: "If boys protest against Israelis building in the Old City, especially around Silwan, or just against harassment, the

Israelis take photos ... and if a protester is seen with a black T-shirt, for example, they arrest all the boys with black T-shirts. It's harassment, but what can we do, we still protest."

If things are bad here, why don't your families move away somewhere else...to the West Bank, say?

Again, all talk at once.

Taseem, the volunteer: "Let me explain what they are saying. Their families know that if they moved away from Jerusalem and went somewhere on the West Bank, to a place like Ramallah say, they would lose their Jerusalem residency and all their rights. That's why they stay put. But the West Bank is very close here and things like Beit Hanina* have happened a lot here. You have examples of houses where the house is in the West Bank and the gardens are in Jerusalem ... and this has all happened without any building permits. It is one rule for them, another for us."

Fida, our Tamer liaison: "I live in Ramallah mostly, but I still have Jerusalem residency. My mom lives in Jerusalem. The worst part is coming into Jerusalem from Ramallah. The Qalandia checkpoint is hard. It can take an hour sometimes, just to get

BEIT HANINA

Beit Hanina is a Palestinian neighborhood in East Jerusalem. It is on the road to Ramallah, 5 miles or 8 kilometers north of central Jerusalem. After the 1967 Six-Day War, the Israelis occupied the West Bank, including Beit Hanina. They also expanded the boundaries of Jerusalem to include the eastern section of Beit Hanina, now known as Beit Hanina al-Jadid. In 1980 this was formalized.

After the Second Intifada in 1992, Israel began to build the Separation Wall, which separates the Jerusalem section of Beit Hanina from the West Bank, isolating it from other Palestinians. The route of the Separation Wall near the town is part of the 10% that is a concrete wall. The area has sometimes been the scene of clashes between the Israeli security forces and Palestinians. On April 18, 2012, a Palestinian family, the Natshehs, was evicted from two houses after an Israeli court decision that the land was owned by settlers. These disputes continue to this day.

through, whereas from Ramallah to Beit Hanina takes five minutes.

The problem with Qalandia is not just that it is a checkpoint. It is a bottleneck of extremely crowded roads. Chaos rules there. It creates problems between Palestinians. The ones from Ramallah see the ones from Jerusalem as the problem and vice versa. It makes conflict between us."

Civic responsibility poster

Protest against confiscation of Palestinian property

TO OUR READERS: THE YOUNG MATTER

We undertook this journey to occupied Palestine because we wanted to see how the situation was affecting the children and young people living there. We knew that Palestine is occupied by Israel and we knew that human rights and occupation do not go together. Knowing is one thing. Crossing borders and being there is another, and it was the experience of being there that has affected us profoundly. Seeing the occupation, with its checkpoints, the Separation Wall, settlements, armed and menacing soldiers, tanks and fighter jets, is understanding the reality, not just knowing about it.

The young people we found there are just like you in many respects. However, they live entirely different lives. Circumstances dictate everything. These young people are caught up in difficult, stressful, and sometimes life-threatening situations. They have voices just like you, but they are not often heard. They matter, as you matter. Having a voice that is listened to means that you matter.

Some of the things you have read may have shocked or surprised you. For example, one of them said "And Jewish people should go where they belong. Russians in Russia, Germans in Germany." This may sound uncompromising, but he went on to say that "any Jewish person that stays must teach their children that they are not the best people, not God's people. We are all the same under God. The same." The way that the country is divided along cultural and religious fault-lines has a profound effect on how both the Palestinians and the Israelis think of themselves and of the "other," and this is one of the tragedies of the situation.

The young people in this book are neither heroes nor villains, nor do they want to be regarded as victims.

Schoolgirls in Hebron

These young people have shared aspects of their lives with us and with you, and this has, it is hoped, breached their isolation by allowing them to reach out to you.

By reading this book we hope you have gained some insight into what is a very long-running and complex situation.

We found young people willing and needing to speak about the weight and the effects of the occupation. Young people who were humbling, but not humbled, informative and informed, gracious and graced with courage, insights, and intelligence, baffled and hurt and at times angry, but, most surprisingly of all, we found young people who almost universally radiated inner strength and optimism, who see a better future for their done-down, weary, seemingly forgotten land—the *al ard* of their ancestors.

We leave you with what one of these young people said to us.

Aya, aged 12, at the Tamer Institute, Ramallah:

"My grandfather used to say, 'The house is our father's and the strangers came to kick us out.' Do you understand?"

Palestinian child worker,
Old City, Jerusalem

TIMELINE OF THE PALESTINIAN-ISRAELI CONFLICT

What follows is a brief outline of a very complex history and current situation. There are references in the pages that follow that offer more detailed history and analysis.

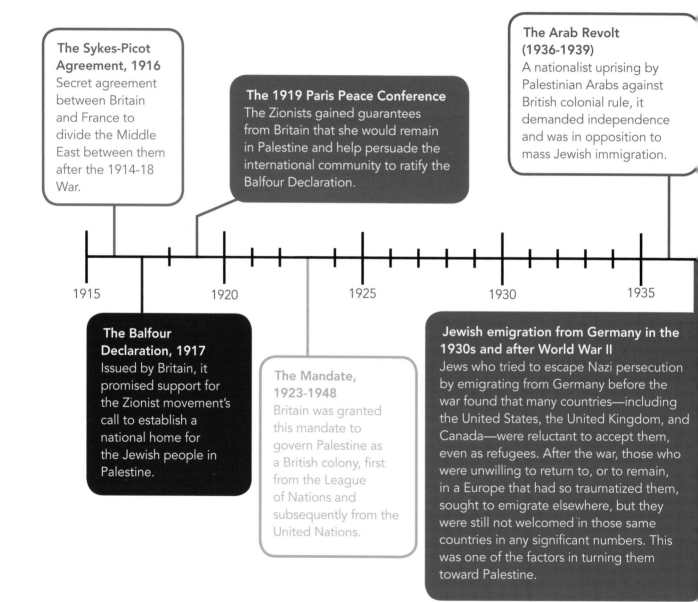

The Sykes-Picot Agreement, 1916
Secret agreement between Britain and France to divide the Middle East between them after the 1914-18 War.

The 1919 Paris Peace Conference
The Zionists gained guarantees from Britain that she would remain in Palestine and help persuade the international community to ratify the Balfour Declaration.

The Arab Revolt (1936-1939)
A nationalist uprising by Palestinian Arabs against British colonial rule, it demanded independence and was in opposition to mass Jewish immigration.

1915 1920 1925 1930 1935

The Balfour Declaration, 1917
Issued by Britain, it promised support for the Zionist movement's call to establish a national home for the Jewish people in Palestine.

The Mandate, 1923-1948
Britain was granted this mandate to govern Palestine as a British colony, first from the League of Nations and subsequently from the United Nations.

Jewish emigration from Germany in the 1930s and after World War II
Jews who tried to escape Nazi persecution by emigrating from Germany before the war found that many countries—including the United States, the United Kingdom, and Canada—were reluctant to accept them, even as refugees. After the war, those who were unwilling to return to, or to remain, in a Europe that had so traumatized them, sought to emigrate elsewhere, but they were still not welcomed in those same countries in any significant numbers. This was one of the factors in turning them toward Palestine.

TIMELINE OF THE PALESTINIAN-ISRAELI CONFLICT

The Jewish Insurgency in Palestine, 1944-1947
This was an armed campaign by Jewish groups, in the main directed at British forces and officials. There were several Zionist paramilitary organizations that operated in Mandate Palestine between 1931 and 1948. The two most active were the Irgun, an offshoot of an older and larger Jewish paramilitary organization, Haganah. Irgun members were absorbed into the Israel Defense Forces at the start of the 1948 Arab-Israel war. The Irgun was described as a terrorist organization by the United Nations and by the British and United States governments. Among the operations they carried out were the bombing of the King David Hotel in Jerusalem on July 22nd 1946, which killed 91 people, and the massacre that took place in Deir Yassin, a Palestinian Arab village, on April 9th 1948, killing 120 people.

The Stern Gang, or Lehi, another extremist Zionist organization, was founded by a former leader of the Irgun. Their terrorist activities also extended beyond Palestine, and they were responsible for assassinating the British Minister of State in Cairo in November, 1944.

continued on next page

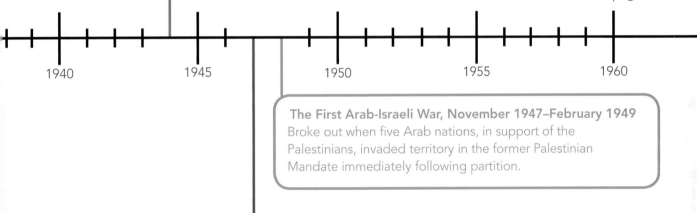

1940 1945 1950 1955 1960

The First Arab-Israeli War, November 1947–February 1949
Broke out when five Arab nations, in support of the Palestinians, invaded territory in the former Palestinian Mandate immediately following partition.

Partition, 1948
State of Israel declared in May 1948 (United Nations Resolution 181(II)). Hundreds of thousands of Palestinians forcibly removed from homes, towns, and cities, becoming refugees.

United Nations Resolution 194, December 1948
The UN passed a resolution that called on Israel to allow the return of refugees. The resolution was, and continues to be, ignored by Israel.

YOUNG PALESTIANS SPEAK

The Six-Day War of 1967
In the 1960's the Palestinians became more active in the struggle against the occupation, and demanded to be recognized as a distinct nation. The Palestinian Liberation Organization (PLO) were committed to the use of armed struggle if necessary. Hostilities between Israel and the Arab countries supporting Palestinians escalated, and on June 1, 1967, Israel declared war.

After the Six-Day War
Israel captured the Sinai Peninsula from Egypt, the Golan Heights from Syria, and the West Bank from Jordan, causing another wave of refugees.

　　The political consequences of Israel's victory were less clear-cut. A debate in Israel was won by the expansionists, and the rapid building of Jewish settlements in the occupied territories followed.

| 1965 | 1970 | 1975 | 1980 | 1985 |

The First Intifada (Uprising), December, 1987
A spontaneous uprising of men, women, and children began in Gaza in December, 1987, in the Jabaliya Refugee Camp in the Gaza Strip, when an Israeli truck crashed into two vans carrying Palestinian workers, killing four of them. This event sparked rebellions throughout the occupied territories, and lasted four to six years.

TIMELINE OF THE PALESTINIAN-ISRAELI CONFLICT

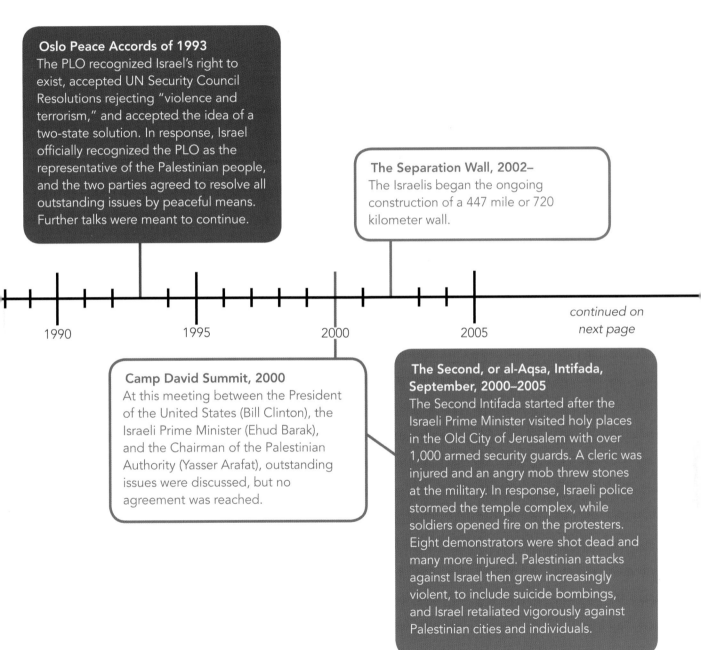

Oslo Peace Accords of 1993
The PLO recognized Israel's right to exist, accepted UN Security Council Resolutions rejecting "violence and terrorism," and accepted the idea of a two-state solution. In response, Israel officially recognized the PLO as the representative of the Palestinian people, and the two parties agreed to resolve all outstanding issues by peaceful means. Further talks were meant to continue.

The Separation Wall, 2002–
The Israelis began the ongoing construction of a 447 mile or 720 kilometer wall.

1990   1995   2000   2005

continued on next page

Camp David Summit, 2000
At this meeting between the President of the United States (Bill Clinton), the Israeli Prime Minister (Ehud Barak), and the Chairman of the Palestinian Authority (Yasser Arafat), outstanding issues were discussed, but no agreement was reached.

The Second, or al-Aqsa, Intifada, September, 2000–2005
The Second Intifada started after the Israeli Prime Minister visited holy places in the Old City of Jerusalem with over 1,000 armed security guards. A cleric was injured and an angry mob threw stones at the military. In response, Israeli police stormed the temple complex, while soldiers opened fire on the protesters. Eight demonstrators were shot dead and many more injured. Palestinian attacks against Israel then grew increasingly violent, to include suicide bombings, and Israel retaliated vigorously against Palestinian cities and individuals.

YOUNG PALESTINIANS SPEAK

Gaza, December 2008– January 2009
Hamas observed a six-month ceasefire on the understanding that Israel would relax the controls of the Gaza borders. Israel did not do this, and conflict in Gaza erupted again when Palestinian militiamen began firing missiles into Israel. Israel retaliated with eight days of heavy aerial bombing. A ceasefire was called in January, 2009.

Gaza, November 2012
Tensions remained high between Israel and the Occupied Territories, especially in Gaza, and in November Israel launched an eight-day military operation in Gaza. Both sides blamed each other for the violence. Human Rights Watch and the UN maintained that both sides had violated the rules of war by targeting civilian populations.

2005   2010   2015   2020

Sharm el-Sheikh Summit, 2005
Palestinian President Mahmoud Abbas and Israeli Prime Minister Ariel Sharon agreed to stop all acts of violence and discussed a "Roadmap for Peace" proposed by the United States, the European Union, Russia, and the United Nations. These discussions led nowhere.

The Gaza conflict, Summer 2014
After several months of rising tensions, an Israeli airstrike killed seven Hamas militants on July 7th. Hamas launched 40 rockets, and Israel began Operation Protective Edge against Gaza. Seven weeks of Israeli bombardment followed, along with an invasion of ground troops. Israeli forces withdrew on August 5th. On August 26, an open-ended ceasefire was announced. (See pages 61–75.)

The Blockade of Gaza and its consequences, 2005–
In 2005, Israel withdrew its settlers and all troops from Gaza. In 2006 Hamas won democratic elections in Gaza. Israel refused to recognize Hamas because Hamas's charter does not recognize the State of Israel. They maintained that security on the Gaza border could not be guaranteed. The Israeli military took complete control of all access by air, land, and sea. Egypt also formally sealed her borders with Gaza, and economic sanctions against Gaza were instituted. All traffic, human or otherwise, into and out of Gaza is now controlled by the Israeli military.

REFERENCES

FILMS

Five Broken Cameras, documentary, Burnat, E (Palestinian) & Davidi, G (Israeli), 2012

Occupation of the American Mind, documentary, Media Education Foundation, 2016

The Stones Cry Out, documentary, Perni, J., 2013

War Child, Children of Gaza, documentary, Neuman, J., 2010

Waltz with Bashir, animated documentary, Folman, A. (Israeli), 2008

WEBSITES

American Friends Service Committee: "The American Friends Service Committee (AFSC) is a Quaker organization that promotes lasting peace with justice, as a practical expression of faith in action."
http://www.afsc.org/resource/israel's-settlement-policy-occupied-palestinian-territory

Amnesty International: The report "Troubled Waters—Palestinians Denied Fair Access To Water," published by Amnesty International in October 2009, details the extent to which Palestinians in the Occupied Palestinian Territories do not have access to adequate, safe water supplies.
http://www.amnesty.eu/en/news/statements-reports/region/middle-east-gulf-states/troubled-waters--palestinians-denied-fair-access-to-water-digest-0420/#.V726n2UQL8s
See also an Amnesty International report on the Occupied Palestinian Territories and Israel:
https://www.amnesty.org/en/countries/middle-east-and-north-africa/israel-and-occupied-palestinian-territories/report-israel-and-occupied-palestinian-territories/

B'Tselem: "The Israeli Information Center for Human Rights in the Occupied Territories was established in February 1989 by a group of prominent academics, attorneys, journalists, and Knesset members. It endeavors to document and educate the Israeli public and policymakers about human rights violations in the Occupied Territories, combat the phenomenon of denial prevalent among the Israeli public, and help create a human rights culture in Israel."
http://www.btselem.org/about_btselem

Breaking the Silence: "[A]n organization of veteran combatants who have served in the Israeli military since the start of the Second Intifada [2000] and have taken it upon themselves to expose the Israeli public to the reality of everyday life in the Occupied Territories. We endeavor to stimulate public debate about the price paid for a reality in which young soldiers face a civilian population on a daily basis, and are engaged in the control of that population's everyday life."

http://www.breakingthesilence.org.il

The British Palestine Friendship and Twinning Network: Sebastiya is twinned with Hanwell (a town in the London Borough of Ealing, west London) in the UK. It was the people of Hanwell who raised in the British Parliament the issue of raw sewage from the Israeli settlement being pumped onto the village fields.

http://www.twinningwithpalestine.net/about.html

Burj al Luq Luq Community Center, East Jerusalem: http://www.burjalluqluq.org/home/

The Encyclopaedia Brittanica: The EB describes the history of the Irgun, the Jewish right wing underground movement:
https://www.britannica.com/topic/Irgun-Zvai-Leumi and also of the Stern Gang, the Zionist extremist organization:
https://www.britannica.com/topic/Stern-Gang

Hebron Youth Centre:
http://ps.unleashingideas.org/users/hebron-youth-development-resource-center-ydrc#sthash.xV5idido.dpuf

Human Rights Watch, 2001 report: https://www.hrw.org/reports/2001/israel/hebron6-04.htm

If Americans Knew: What every American needs to know about Israel/Palestine: "The mission of If Americans Knew is to inform and educate the American public on issues of major significance that are unreported, underreported, or misreported in the American media."

http://www.ifamericansknew.org/about_us/

Interlink Publishing: A Massachustts-based independent publishing house with a large selection of books relating to Israel/Palestine, including Palestinian fiction-in-translation, poetry, history and politics, biography, and books on Palestinian art and culture. www.interlinkbooks.com

Michael Rosen: Michael is an author and poet. Read his poem: "Promised Land"
http://michaelrosenblog.blogspot.co.uk/2014/08/poem-promised-land.html

Miko Peled: Miko Peled is the son of an Israeli General. In addition to his book, *The General's Son*, he writes a blog "dedicated to tearing down the separation wall and transforming the Israeli apartheid system into a secular democracy, where Israelis and Palestinians will live as equal citizens."
https://mikopeled.com/?blogsub=confirming#blog_subscription-3

Mondoweiss: "[A]n independent website devoted to informing readers about developments in Israel/Palestine and related US foreign policy. We provide news and analysis unavailable through the mainstream media regarding the struggle for Palestinian human rights. Founded in 2006 as a personal blog of journalist Philip Weiss, Mondoweiss grew inside the progressive Jewish community and has become a critical resource for the movement for justice for Palestinians."
http://mondoweiss.net

Netketabi: "Meaning "My Netbook" in Arabic, is a multi-dimensional educational solution that aims to build the competencies of Palestinian youth. ....'
http://psdpal.org/index.php/programs/netketabi

The Palestine Monitor: "The Palestine Monitor was established in December 2000, after the start of the Second Intifada... Dr. Mustafa Barghouthi established The Palestine Monitor to be a counterweight to the bias against Palestine found in many international news sources ... Our aim is transparent: to present the Palestinian perspective."
http://palestinemonitor.org

Raif al Badawi: https://www.amnesty.org.uk/issues/Raif-Badawi

TAMER Institute for Community Education: "[A]n educational non-governmental organization established in 1989. Working with children and young adults in the fields of reading promotion, expressive arts; reading, writing, art, drama and theatre. The publishing unit program publishes stories for children and young adults in addition to translations of international literary works into Arabic, the publications focus on opening questions for children and flourishing their imagination. Tamer is a winner of many international awards such as the Astrid Lindgren Memorial Award (ALMA) 2009, the world's largest award for children's and young adult's literature ..."
http://www.tamerinst.org/about-us

United Nations Educational, Scientific and Cultural Organisation UNESCO: Education for All Monitoring Report
http://www.unesco.org/new/fileadmin/MULTIMEDIA/HQ/ED/pdf/gmr2011-part2-ch3.pdf

United Nations Independent Commission of Inquiry on the 2014 Gaza Conflict: http://www.ohchr.org/en/NewsEvents/Pages/DisplayNews.aspx?NewsID=16119&LangID=E

A useful article on the Separation Wall: https://electronicintifada.net/blogs/ben-white/did-israeli-apartheid-wall-really-stop-suicide-bombings

BOOKS

Chomsky, Noam. *Power and Terror*. London: Pluto Press, 2011.

Chomsky, Noam and Ilan Pappé. *Gaza in Crisis*. London: Hamish Hamilton/ Penguin, 2010.

Kapuscinski, Ryszard. *The Other*. London: Verso, 2008.

Keenan, Brigid. *Packing Up*. London: Bloomsbury, 2014.

Montefoire, Simon Sebag. *Jerusalem: The Biography*. London: Orion Books, 2011.

Pappé, Ilan. *The Ethnic Cleansing of Palestine*. London: Oneworld Publications, 2006

Pappé, Ilan. *The Forgotten Palestinians*. Yale. Yale University Publications: 2011

Peled, Miko. *The General's Son: Journey of an Israeli in Palestine*. Charlottesville, VA: Just World Books, 2012

Pilger, John. *The New Rulers of the World*. London: Verso, 2003.

Sabbagh, Karl. *Palestine: A Personal History*. London: Atlantic Books, 2006.

Shlaim, Avi. *Israel and Palestine*. London: Verso, 2009.

Shehadeh, Raja. *Palestinian Walks: Notes on a Vanishing Landscape*. London: Profile Books, 2008.

Shehadeh, Raja. *Occupation Diaries*. London: Profile Books, 2012.

Shehadeh, Raja. *When the Bulbul Stopped Singing*. London: Profile Books, 2003.

Books For Students:

Barakat, Ibtisam. *Tasting the Sky: A Palestinian Childhood*. New York: Farrar, Straus and Giroux, 2007.

Carter, Anne Laurel. *The Shepherd's Granddaughter*. Canada: Groundwood Books, 2008.

Laird, Elizabeth. *A Little Piece of Ground*. London: Macmillan, 2003.

Naidoo, Beverley. *The Other Side of Truth*. London: Puffin Books, 2000.

Sutcliff, William. *The Wall*. London: Walker Books, 2013.

Whitesides, Barbara. *Sugar Comes from

REFERENCES

Arabic: A Beginner's Guide to Arabic Letters and Words. Northampton: Interlink Books, 2009.

MORE INTERLINK BOOKS ABOUT PALESTINE AND PALESTINIANS

FOR STUDENTS AND FAMILIES:
Food, Art, and Culture:

Abu-Ghazeleh, Waleed. *Love Wins: Palestinian Perseverance Behind Walls.* 2013.

Kalla, Joudie. *Palestine on a Plate: Memories from My Mother's Kitchen.* 2016.

Weir, Shelagh. *Palestinian Costume.* 2009.

Szepesi, Stefan. *Walking Palestine: 25 Journeys into the West Bank.* 2012.

Poetry and Fiction:

Al-Barghouti, Tamim. *In Jerusalem and Other Poems.* 2017.

Darwish, Mahmoud; translated by Mohammad Shaheen. *Almond Blossoms and Beyond.* 2009.

Jayyusi, Salma Khadra. *Tales of Juha. Classic Arab Folk Humor.* 2007.

Sleem, Jamal. *Abu Jmeel's Daughter and Other Stories: Arab Folk Tales from Palestine and Lebanon.* 2002.

FOR PARENTS AND TEACHERS:

Bennis, Phyllis. *Understanding the Palestinian-Israeli Conflict.* 2015.

Isaksen, Runo; translated by Kari Dickson. *Literature and War: Conversations with Israeli and Palestinian Writers.* 2009.

Shaheen, Mariam. *Palestine: A Guide.* 2006.

Tamari, Salim and Issam Nassar (eds). *The Storyteller of Jerusalem: The Life and Times of Wasif Jawhariyyeh, 1904-1948.* 2013